FAMOUS FORD V-8S

FAMOUS
FORD V-8S

BY LORIN SORENSEN

Left: *A cover photo for* Ford News *featuring a new '40 Mercury V-8* Town Sedan *with an admirer and some Detroit Lions football players. Their team was destined to be owned by William Clay Ford, son of Edsel Ford, the man who created the famous Mercury line.*

SILVERADO PUBLISHING COMPANY, ST. HELENA, CALIFORNIA
and Ten Speed Press, Berkeley, California

This is a Silverado Publishing Company book.

Written and produced by Lorin Sorensen

Published by Silverado Publishing Company
P.O. Box 393
St. Helena, California 94574

Typesetting by Ellen Peters

Cover art by Brian Nash

Photo production by David Fetherston

Edited by Cliff and Cara Swartz

ISBN NO. 1-58008-426-5

Printed in Hong Kong by Global Interprint,
Santa Rosa, California.

Available from Ten Speed Press, Box 7123,
Berkeley, California, 94707. www.tenspeed.com

Distributed in Australia by Simon & Schuster
Australia, in Canada by Ten Speed Press Canada,
in New Zealand by Southern Publishers Group,
in South Africa by Real Books, in Southeast Asia
by Berkeley Books, and in the United Kingdom
and Europe by Airlift Book Company.

First printing, 2002

1 2 3 4 5 6 7 8 9 10 – 07 06 05 04 03 02

New friends in a '36 Ford Convertible Sedan at an Oakland, California, convention.

ACKNOWLEDGMENTS

It is very much appreciated that many of the Ford stylists and engineers who were there when the early V-8s were created, have left us their stories. For this we owe a debt of gratitude to Owen Bombard, David Crippen, Mike Davis, and others who had the foresight to interview them for the Oral History project at the Henry Ford Museum Research Center.

Also, a special thanks to Dan Brooks, Ellen Peters, David Fetherston, and Ed Spagnola, who were particularly helpful with this book.
LORIN SORENSEN

— CONTENTS —

Monte Mansfield, right, the Ford dealer in Tuscon, Arizona, celebrates the arrival of his first 1932 Ford V-8, a Tudor Sedan. It was an event repeated across the U.S. as dealers at last had a replacement for the Model A.

Opposite: The first look at the sensational new '32 Ford V-8 at a London showroom. The engineering was all Henry Ford's. Luckily, he left the car's styling to his son Edsel.

The success of the V-8 engine helped Ford sales hit the million mark in 1935. To stir up some publicity, "Miss V-8 Radio Girl" is pictured touring downtown Houston, Texas, in a gorgeous '35 Phaeton detailed in factory cream show color with optional chrome-plated wheels.

Opposite: An evening crowd admires a sporty new '36 Ford Cabriolet at the elegant Freitas & Co., showroom in Porto, Portugal — unaware that it would be their last chance to buy. Fords for here were built at the Barcelona, Spain, plant, which was soon seized by Leftists and forced to make military trucks for the 1936-39 Spanish Civil War.

War was in the air so Edsel Ford and his chief designer Bob Gregorie gave the '41 Ford styling an aviation theme. This sales photo taken at a hanger near Detroit, makes the comparison between fun, airplanes, and the *sporty new* Super Deluxe Convertible Club Coupe.

Opposite: *An early Ford color photo shows in revealing detail a 1940 Ford Standard Tudor Sedan body being 'decked' with a V-8 chassis at the Dearborn assembly plant.*

INTRODUCTION

Edsel Ford

Henry Ford gave little credit to his son Edsel for contributing so much to his own great success. Not just as his most able business executive but as his best automotive stylist.

Edsel was Henry and Clara Ford's only child. Born in Detroit in 1893, he showed an early interest in art, and by his teens began sketching automobiles. As a young man he went to work for his father, continuing his interest in auto design and often presenting ideas to make the hot-selling Model T even better. But his father wasn't interested. So, in 1922, ostensibly to get the boy off his back and give him "something to play with," Henry Ford bought the troubled Lincoln Motor Company from the Leland family and turned its operations over to Edsel.

It was purely business, but also a happy solution. The respected Leland's were rescued from total failure and Edsel was out of the way to vent his styling frustrations on the big, stodgy Lincolns, which he did to perfection. He soon revamped the Lincolns into one of America's most prestigious and beautiful automobiles.

Edsel was so successful in turning around Lincoln that many wondered what he might have done with a free hand at Ford. "I think if Edsel had taken over the company . . . and run it according to his ideas," mused the old Model T engineer Joe Galamb, "it would have been better. We would have been on the new model before the Chevrolet could get ahead of us. It was too late in '28 to make the model change (to Model A). It should have been done in '24 or '25."

At 29, Edsel was a young man when he took over at Lincoln. But he quickly became well-schooled in the automobile business and matured into a refined gentleman, perfectly suited for his new job. His own stable of cars included a big, fast, Hispano-Suiza, and custom Packards and Cadillacs. A. J. Lepine, his personal secretary for 25 years, recalled that Edsel "was totally immersed in cars, especially ones with the latest design," and that he arrived to work each day at the Lincoln offices in a special chauffeured Lincoln.

Edsel was soft-spoken, quite a sportsman, and a "fine dresser," noted Lepine. "He had sports clothes for all occasions. . . . He was a yachtsman and for a few years was actively interested in motorboat racing on the Detroit River."

Edsel married Eleanor Lowthian Clay in 1916 and their four children were Henry II, Benson, Josephine, and William Clay Ford. The family estate was at Lake St. Claire Shores near Detroit and even in the twenties Edsel had an impressive annual income of about $3 million.

At Lincoln, Edsel developed a formula for auto design that would serve him well in the years to come. The routine was to have the custom body suppliers such as Murphy, Brewster and Holbrook submit their ideas, then he would have them, "add a little here — take off a little there" . . . until he had just the distinctive car he was looking for.

All this time Edsel never personally drew a line. He didn't have to. He had such a natural eye for detail and was so respected by the trained stylists on the drawing boards that his suggestions became their designs.

He did a fine job with the Lincoln. Even his father, who was a chassis man and didn't care much how a car looked, approved and gave him the 1928-31 Model A Fords to style. Edsel made the front-ends resemble that of each year's new Lincoln, and then worked with the outside suppliers to design the bodies.

It was the same with the sporty new Ford V-8 styling. Only this time the often mean-spirited Henry Ford put obstacles in Edsel's way, making him improvise and never giving him a real design department until 1935. It was his father's way of making Edsel tough. Fortunately, Edsel had as his chief stylist the brilliant E. T. "Bob" Gregorie. Together they would find a way around the old man, creating some of the most memorable car designs of all time.

It was beautiful teamwork but it all came to an end when Edsel died suddenly in 1943. Sadly, his father never recognized that one of Ford Motor Company's greatest talents was his own son.
— *LORIN SORENSEN*

Edsel Ford found inspiration for the new '32 Ford styling from his own beautifully-proportioned Lincolns — like this stunning Murphy-bodied *KB-12 Roadster.*

". . . Edsel's particular purpose was to expand a better taste in the Ford product — a higher plane taste . . ."E. T. "BOB" GREGORIE, FORD CHIEF STYLIST

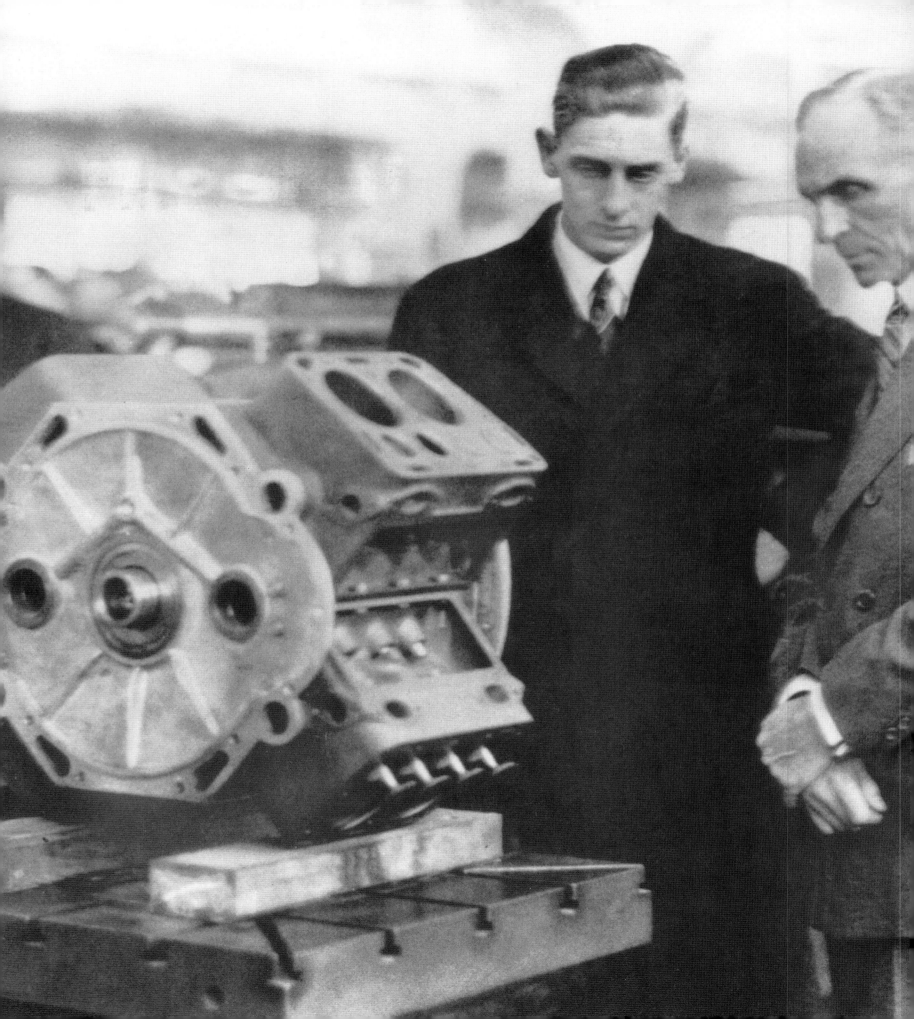

HENRY FORD REINVENTS THE V-8

Henry Ford was no stranger to the V-8. In fact, he had been in full production of this type engine since 1922 when he took over the Lincoln Motor Car Company. It was only logical then that the big car's Leland-designed, precision-built V-8 would play a role in the automaker's thinking as he brooded over the inevitable – a successor to his world famous Model T 4-cylinder engine.

As lagging sales showed, the Model T was on its way out. Ford was already thinking seriously about a compact, smooth-running "8" that could be mass-produced cheaply. Something like a lighter version of the engines in his luxury Lincolns. But Henry Ford was not an imitator. He wanted something completely new and revolutionary – something he alone would invent – an engine that would surprise everyone and sell his next generation of cars. Cars we now know as the Model A Fords.

One day he came across a steam-driven airplane-type "X-engine" that was installed in a speedboat. He became intrigued by it and ordered his top experimental engineer Eugene "Gene" Farkas to work on the idea for a possible automobile engine. Together, they changed the design from air-cooled to water-cooled. By 1925, they had one of the engines running, with steel pistons, roller main bearings, and a supercharger built into the flywheel. But the Ford X-8, shaped like a radial airplane engine, was heavy, and tricky to build. When they stuck it in a chassis and gave it a road test the bottom spark plugs running along in the dust, fouled out. Other serious problems developed and the X-8 experiment was scrapped.

After a fantastic run of nearly two decades, the Model T had to be replaced. Competitors were bringing out cars with faster, smoother 6-cylinder engines and cutting heavily into sales. Finally, in May 1927, Henry Ford stopped production

Left: **Henry Ford with his experimental X-8 engine in November 1926. By now he realized that the radial design, with its road-hugging spark plugs subject to fouling, was not practical. What he learned was soon put to good use, however, when he developed his own kind of low-priced V-8 as its successor.**

of the Model T forever and began a crash project to quickly bring out its successor – the 1928 Model A. There was no time to develop an ingenious V-8 engine, so what proved to be the very timely, sensational Model A, simply got a hotter, improved "Four".

Still, the competition bore down. Then came the Wall Street crash and the beginnings of the Great Depression. Within a couple of years, it looked like the Model A was going the way of the old "T", only much quicker. Something had to be done – and quickly!

One of Ford's engineers, Fred Thoms, was there when the big decision was made. He would later remark, "The day General Motors went from a four to a six Mr. Ford came in and said, 'We're going to go from a four to an eight, because the Chevrolet is going to a six'. . . . He went on to tell me, 'Now, you try to get all the old eight-cylinder engines that you can.' I guess we picked up about nine in scrap yards, old cars, and all over. We washed them up and laid them out to get some kind of idea . Those eight-cylinder engines were all in one or two pieces. The cylinder block was bolted to the crankshaft . . . One of them was in two halves. They were very costly, and you just couldn't make them cheap enough for a cheap car. That is why we went to the idea of making a V-8 cylinder block in one piece – for cheapness."

Ford engineer William F. Pioch was one of the engineers who worked on that first engine. He thought it was more the idea of speed that led Henry Ford to the lightweight V-8. "In order to get power to accomplish this speed," he said, "a four-cylinder engine would get too big in the bore and the stroke was too heavy. You could do a better job with an eight-cylinder. Of course, he was right on that because everybody has followed suit since then. . . ."

It was mid-1930 and with a sense of urgency Henry Ford directed another of his engineers, Arnold Soth, to start laying out ideas from the old V-8 engines. Ford's personal engineer Carl Schultz soon joined Soth in secret. Within a short time, the project was moved to the seclusion of Henry Ford's new Greenfield Village collection of historic American buildings in Dearborn. Here the engineers were given

Five of the key men who carried out Henry Ford's orders in developing the 1932 Ford V-8 are pictured at the Ford Engineering Laboratory in Dearborn. Left to right are Ford chief engineer, Laurence "Larry" Sheldrick; Edsel's production assistant, John Crawford; chief body engineer Joe Galamb; production manager Peter E. Martin, and experimental engineer Gene Farkas. All were longtime Ford men.

Thomas Edison's reconstructed old Ft. Meyers, Florida, workshop where they could work without notice.

Soth soon left the project and trusted engineers Fred Thoms, Ray Laird, and Emil Zoerlein joined Schultz. "Mr. Ford was vitally interested in a one-piece casting of the cylinder block," recalled Zoerlein. "It had to be one piece, definitely. . . . that was about July of 1930 . . . Mr. Ford told me what he wanted. He wanted a distributor mounted on the front end of the engine and driven directly off the camshaft. He said, 'You'll probably run into a lot of opposition on that, but that is what I want, and that is what is going to go on this engine.' Mr. Ford came in two or three times a day (and) kept everybody away from it but the three of us and himself . . ."

It was a mystery known only to the auto genius why the V-8 project was carried out under such crude conditions at Edison's old steam-driven shop. Just a few hundred yards away sat his world-class engineering building with all of its facilities. And not far away was his Lincoln Motor Company plant with its experienced hands already making V-8s. "There was nobody allowed down at the Village," said Thoms, "or near that engine. I don't think Mr. Sorensen or Mr. Martin (Ford production chiefs) were down there either. Everybody was kept out of there because it was a very secret job." Even Chief Engineer, Lawrence "Larry" Sheldrick was left out of the early stages of the V-8 engine development. "Mr. Sheldrick came in after the engine was laid out," said Pioch. "It was unusual for the chief engineer not to come in before that, but that . . . was Mr. Ford's idea."

Sheldrick was finally let in on the secret project in early 1931 and while he didn't like being kept in the dark, shrugged it off as just another one of Mr. Ford's strange ways. "You could usually tell when he really intended to do something with a job because he would take it off and hide it. A lot of these things he did that he wasn't too serious about he would have done right out in the open," he explained.

By the time Sheldrick got involved, the project had been moved into his big, fully equipped Ford Engineering Building where the last problems of producing an inexpensive V-8 engine block all in one piece were worked out.

Fred Thoms was put in charge of fabricating the experimental engines. "There were a lot of pattern makers on that block, because Mr. Ford wanted to get it going fast," he told an oral history interviewer. "We would almost have a motor going within a week. That is — a week from the drawing to starting the motor . . . Mr. Ford used to be there with us until eleven o'clock at night. He would watch things very closely and make suggestions as we went along. . . . He was thorough and wanted everything done exactly right. . . . He suggested all the things that he wanted done. . . . We would try it out on a test or on a car and if it didn't work out, we would go to something else."

As the work progressed, one of the most important men assigned to the job was chief experimental engineer Gene Farkas. Farkas remembered that his boss Henry Ford cared little for blueprints and developed the V-8 layout mostly by studying designs the men drew on the blackboard. "He would know enough about it," he said, "to determine whether that particular idea suited him or not."

Emil Zorelein was always in awe of Henry Ford, who at best had the equivalent of a fifth grade country education. "The uncanny atmosphere about Mr. Ford," recalled the engineer, "was more or less his enthusiasm. He was able to inspire people. . . . It was a combination of his presence, the look in his eye, the determined expression on his face, and still he talked softly . . ."

But when the automaker did make up his mind about something, his men knew that was it! "He (Henry Ford) would never permit a tappet adjustment (on the new V-8)," recalled Sheldrick, "that is, an adjustment for valve clearance. We had to manufacture push rods and valves of proper length so no adjustment was required. . . . That was an enormous manufacturing problem., but we learned how to do it . . ."

It took more than a year before Henry Ford was satisfied that he had a workable V-8 engine. It was the one originally worked up from scratch by Carl Schultz.

Four of the engines were built and installed in revamped Model A's for testing out on the road during the late winter of 1931. Sheldrick thought Edsel Ford "was very much for this V-8" as far as innovation, but was concerned about the suddenness and poor test results and ". . . fearful that we would have trouble. And we did have trouble."

But Henry Ford pressed on. Most of the bugs in the V-8 were worked out, and then it became a question of getting it quickly out in the market.

Getting the V-8 into mass production, overcoming the obstacles of casting the engine block in a single piece and nearly running the company out of cash is one of the industry's great legends. But, as always, the automaker had one last trick up his sleeve. If all had failed, he was fully prepared to bring out the new V-8 car instead with the optional 4-cylinder "Model B" engine. In fact, the new '32 chassis was designed to accept either engine.

Meanwhile, Edsel Ford was at work styling the all-new Ford V-8s. ◆

Henry Ford worked long hours directing every engineering detail of his new V-8 car, leaving the body designs to his son Edsel.

"... Most of the time I saw Mr. Ford he had a gray suit on; it was a herringbone outfit . . . He always wore a certain type of shoe like kid glove . . . it was very fine and very light . . . He had gray piercing eyes and a sharp expression . . . His line of speech was quick and snappy . . ." GENE FARKAS, FORD EXPERIMENTAL ENGINEER

EDSEL CREATES A LEGEND

*I*ncredibly, throughout the Model A years leading to the dramatic changeover to the V-8 in 1932, Ford Motor Company did not have a real styling department. That is, a roomful of designers who started with a clean slate to style a new car. But it was typical of Henry Ford. He didn't like excessive engineers, managers, or anyone who would try to share his glory—and he especially didn't care for artists. That was one of the tragedies in the relationship with his son Edsel, who he thought was just too sensitive and artistic for the automobile business — and not hard-as-nails like him. So to toughen him up — to see how he'd do on his own — he gave Edsel the difficult job of designing his cars without much of a staff or studio. He had done that with the Lincoln and Model A, and now he would do it with the new V-8.

Edsel chose as his base of operations the Lincoln plant where his father was least likely to interfere with ongoing developments. There Edsel had a few draftsmen and body men who could coordinate ideas with a similar number at the nearby Ford operations.

To get ideas into production at Ford, Edsel had a close working relationship with Joe Galamb. Galamb was a dapper Hungarian who dated back to drawing up the first Model T's. He was also considered a clever "put-togetherer" and was affectionately called "Joe Shitametal" for such expressions as, "you make it outa the shitametal, see, shitametal." Galamb actually came up through the ranks in chassis production and while Henry Ford didn't like his men to have titles, Galamb was known in the thirties as "executive engineer in the body department." Since Model A days his primary job was to coordinate with Briggs, the company's main body supplier.

If Edsel had any real "head of design" on his staff, it was Henry Crecelius. Crecelius was brought in from Brewster Body Company as Edsel's chief engineer at the Lincoln plant. Edsel's practice was to give ideas to Crecelius, who would then develop the design of each new Lincoln model's grille, hood, fenders, bumpers. hubcaps, etc., as part of chassis engineering. From this would come the new Lincoln

coachwork designs supplied primarily by the custom body shops such as Brewster, Locke, and Brunn.

Of course Henry Ford ruled supreme on every detail of the new Ford V-8 chassis (or the workings of any of his cars for that matter), and styling remained secondary to chassis engineering. While the automaker always wanted to originate the chassis ideas, he sometimes listened to others. "I remember Joe Galamb had an idea about that ('32 Ford) frame to make it wide enough so we could eliminate the splash board we had between the running board and body," recalled Gene Farkas, "We formed the frame in such a way that it looked like a splash board . . . That is about as far as he (Henry) went with the body."

"Henry Ford was continually feeding ideas to Farkas," complained Larry Sheldrick, who was often frustrated by the closeness of old Henry and his experimental engineer. "We would pick them up there and if they were feasible we would put them into production." "If he had told Farkas to make a cylinder block out of wood, by God, I think Farkas would have tried it!" Said Farkas in his own account "Mr. Ford was a great believer in trying an idea, no matter how foolish it seemed, just for the experience of it. It didn't make a bit of difference to him whether it was successful or not as long as we tried to find out something nobody else had found out or tried . . ."

As the '32 V-8 chassis evolved, work began on the car's styling.

In January 1931, Edsel hired a bright young designer as an assistant to Henry Crecelius at Lincoln.

His name was Eugene "Bob" Gregorie, a trained naval architect who had worked with Crecelius designing automobile bodies at Brewster. Years later, Gregorie recalled getting the job. "The day before New Year's, I received a telegram from Henry Crecelius to come to work at Fords in Dearborn. . . . My work there involved design sketches for Lincoln cars, Lincoln bodies, custom-type bodies and so on. . . . It was a small group: Mr. Crecelius and two or three body draftsmen and several detailers. Everything was on a very

The first proud showing of a new '32 Ford *Victoria* at the Walter M. Casey sales-room in San Diego, California, attracts an admiring crowd. Edsel's body designs were so beautifully matched with his father's speedy V-8 engines that the '32 models would become all-time American classics.

"The V-8 was a response to the Chevy's Six. Salesmen felt that they needed a smooth engine, and the 4-cylinder was not smooth. The Ford Motor Company tried to increase its power but this shook the car and was clearly not the answer. Ford then devised the V-8." JOHN R. DAVIS, FORD SALES MANAGER

Young and full of ideas, Bob Gregorie was hired at Lincoln in time to add his talents to the '32 Ford design. He understood what Edsel wanted and became his top stylist.

Edsel directed the design of all the Lincolns since 1922 and the entire Model A line before styling the '32 Fords. Amazingly, all this without formal training or a real styling department.

small scale. . . . It was the practice then for Mr. (Edsel) Ford to select from design sketches brought to Detroit by the various body builders (Judkins, Brunn, etc.) for his selection."

In working up front-end designs at Lincoln, Gregorie and the others were in effect developing the lines of the new '32 Ford as well. Said Gregorie, ". . . It was really a miniature Lincoln. . . . The placement of the headlamps, the fender shapes, the radiator contour, and the whole thing was a scaled-down Lincoln."

Once the chassis and front-end design was set, as with Lincoln the Ford body makers were called in to design and produce the coachwork under Edsel's guidance. Briggs was the biggest supplier, designing and producing sedans, cabriolets, roadsters, phaetons, sport coupes, and truck bodies. Murray produced the closed coupes, victorias, and convertible sedans.

Edsel made all the final body design decisions, including the upholstery and colors and also got into areas of engineering. He directed such design details as the instrument panel and steering wheel, the art-deco V-8 hubcaps and the Lincoln-like "corrugated" bumpers. It was a classic combina-

tion, but, if it wasn't for his ability to make the right design decisions quickly, the results could have been much different.

"Old Henry Ford had absolutely no interest in the design and appearance of the car," complained Gregorie, who was just learning the conflicts of father and son. "A lot of the niceties that Edsel Ford wanted to build into the product — he felt were superfluous. He had a mania for simplicity, I mean, plain simplicity."

Gene Farkas had long ago learned who was boss. ". . . I had to be careful when I worked for Edsel Ford," he said, "on account of Mr. (Henry) Ford's feelings that he was supposed to be the directing genius."

It was a strange situation but, always the gentleman, Edsel got the job done in styling the new '32s — and were they beauties!

The first Ford V-8 came off the assembly line on March 9, 1932. By the 29th, every dealer in the U.S. had one to show and on April 2nd, the cars were unveiled to an admiring public. What follows is a record in words and pictures of how it was when one of the most popular American automobiles of all time came out of production and took to the road. ◆

"... It (the 1932 V-8 design) was really a miniature Lincoln ... the placement of the headlamps, the fender shapes, the radiator contour, and the whole thing was a scaled-down Lincoln ... A man doesn't have to be a designer ... He (Edsel) knew when something looked right ..." E. T. "BOB" GREGORIE, FORD CHIEF STYLIST

The '32 Ford V-8's styling kinship with the Lincoln is obvious in this front-end comparison with a *Cabriolet* model. It was the formula for a famous decade-long collaboration of two talents as Gregorie perfected Edsel's ideas.

Phaeton bodies roll down the line toward final assembly at a Ford plant during the summer of 1932.

Right: One of Henry Ford's new V-8 engines meets a chassis at Dearborn in June 1932. For the next 21 years the "Ford flathead" would be one of the industry's great success stories.

Left: Father and son inspect one of the first '32 Ford V-8s assembled at Dearborn.

"The V-8 was the Model B car, in its entirety, except the engine. The car, therefore, was all developed, and we continued to build the Model B, with the Model B four cylinder engine, and in March, put in this V-8 engine..."
LAURENCE SHELDRICK, FORD CHIEF ENGINEER

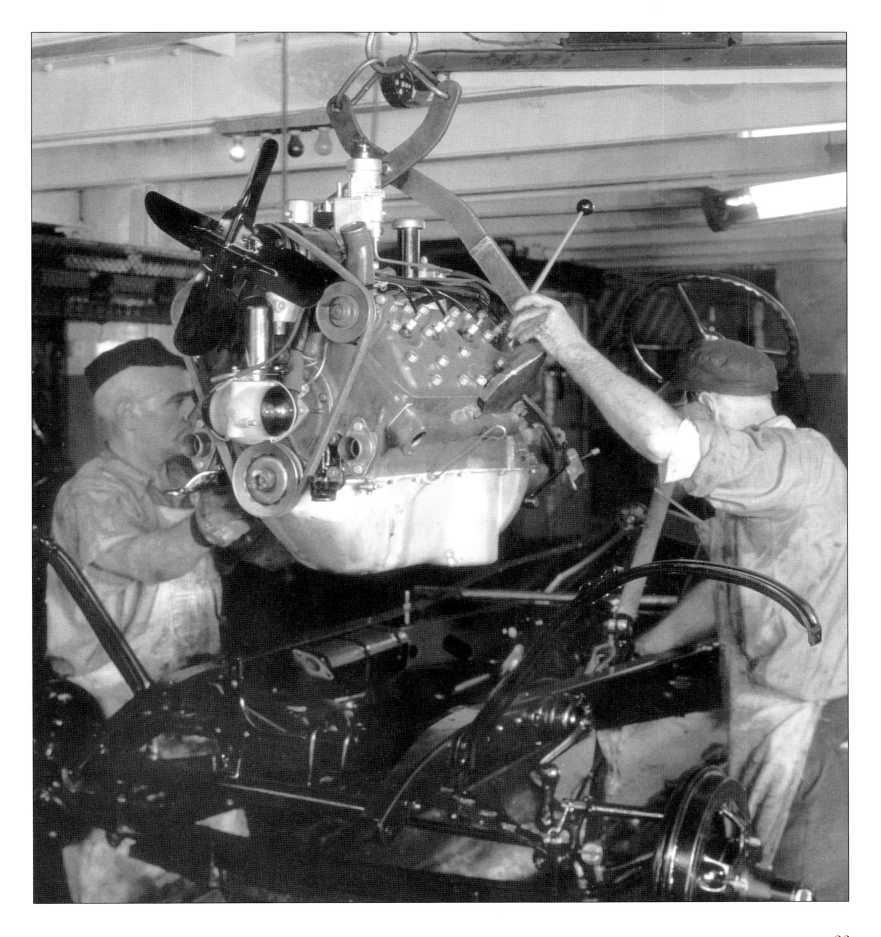

The first Ford V-8s were produced at the Rouge plant in Dearborn, Michigan, March 9, 1932. A crew makes the delicate match of a *Tudor Sedan* body to the separately installed chassis firewall, which was unique to the '32 Fords.

Left: Edsel's objective was to get the very best in Ford coachwork. Here at the Seattle assembly plant, following a 4-cylinder Model BB Truck, a freshly lacquered and pin-striped '32 *Tudor Sedan* body is carefully lowered to a chassis. It was one of the few cars built at the brand new facility which — because of the deepening Depression — was soon closed, never to assemble again.

THE NEW FORD V-8

The Ford 65-horsepower 8-cylinder V-type engine is the first and only engine of its kind to be made available in a low-priced car.

Like all Ford engines, it is simple in design and construction and especially neat in appearance. The two banks of four cylinders each are cast in a single piece with the crankcase, for rigidity, and permanent alignment of cylinders.

The modern trend is reflected in the style of the Ford V-8. The basis of its beauty is the air-flow line, expressive of new speed and power. Streamlines begin at the very front of the car. They are reflected in the windshield, which slants at 10 degrees. The front roof line is rounded, without sun visor. Inside front visors, easily adjustable, are a convenient feature in closed cars for driver and front seat passenger. Top, sides, and rear of the body, all have gracefully curved lines conforming with the air-flow principle.

There are fourteen beautiful body types.

To suit individual preferences, there is a wide choice of colors. Mouldings and stripings are in attractive contrasting, or harmonizing colors, which accentuate the gracefulness of the lines. All color combinations are unusually smart and up-to-the-minute.

The new "4" can also be had in any of the 14 beautiful body types. The new 4-cylinder engine is mounted in rubber and operates smoothly and quietly. It develops 50 horsepower. *Ford News, May 1932*

America fell in love with the snappy '32 Fords. Society matrons pose with the first *Convertible Sedan* model shown at Olympia, Washington.

Right: Curious about Henry Ford's new V-8s, a crowd tries out an exhibit of models, including a *Coupe* and a *Deluxe Phaeton* at a dealer show in Tacoma, Washington. Exciting as they were, the toughest job was winning over 4-cylinder customers who were dubious of V-8 reliability.

" . . . The (early) V-8 didn't perform well. Many vital elements were faulty – the radiator, fuel pump, distributor – while oil consumption was high and there was overheating . . ." JOHN R. DAVIS, FORD SALES MANAGER

One of the first celebrities won over by the new '32 Ford V-8 was boxing champ Max Baer, pictured with his wife and their unpretentious *Standard Tudor Sedan* at the airport in his home town of Sacramento, California. In 1934 he beat Primo Carnera to win the world heavy-weight boxing championship — losing it a year later to Joe Louis. Baer went on to become a Hollywood film regular and radio personality. In later years his son Max Baer, Jr. starred in TV's *The Beverly Hillbillies.*

Right: Built at the Ford assembly plant at Louisville, Kentucky, a handsome *5-window Coupe* sits in a local showroom. It differs from the *Deluxe 3-window* model for this year in the door and window design, painted windshield frame, and no cowl lights. Beyond is one of the new Pickups which came standard with the 4-cylinder engine.

Famed aviator Wiley Post poses with his new '32 Ford *3-window Coupe* at the State Capitol building in Oklahoma City. Murray Corporation of America supplied the bodies for these rakish models with the blind roof quarter and — a first ever for a Ford — front-opening "suicide doors." This was also the first Ford model to get a glove compartment in the dash. Wiley was Will Rogers' pilot when they fatally crashed in Alaska in 1935.

The *Deluxe Roadster* became Edsel's most famous '32 Ford model and was arguably the best executed from the Lincoln design. In time, America's youth would confirm his styling brilliance by searching these beauties out to make the best-looking hotrods of all time.

Right: A '32 Ford 4-cylinder Model B *Roadster* stars in an oil promotion for Union Oil Company in Los Angeles. Note the jazzy lattice-work whitewalls. Quick identification of the '32 Model B was the absence of "V-8" emblems on the hubcaps and headlight bar. The Model A-like optional engine was Henry Ford's hedge in case his V-8 failed to attract customers.

The first 1932 Ford V-8 *Victoria* model built at the Portland, Oregon, assembly plant went to department store magnate Fred Meier of that city. Meier, right, is shown accepting the title from local Ford dealer C. E. Francis. Top of the line for Ford closed models, the deluxe '32 *Victoria* featured a stylish "bustle-back" rear quarter. Split front seat backs gave passengers access to the rear cushion.

MOTOREZE
A BLENDED MOTOR OIL

EASIER ON YOUR MOTOR

Once the problems with the early Ford V-8 engines were sorted out, gentlemen British race drivers, like others around the world, found the speed of the Ford V-8 amazing. A "Jabberwock" race team '32 *Cabriolet* tears through the countryside for a win near Cardiff during the annual Welsh Rally. It was already a road race veteran, less running boards, with a strapped-down hood, and bobbed fenders. The properly attired mechanic rides in the rumble seat for more traction. Right-hand-drive, and fender-mounted parking lights, were distinguishing features of the 1932 Fords built at Dagenham, England.

Right: Four-cylinder "Model B" Ford Cabriolets belonging to the Jabberwock (means "nonsense") race team show their speed and agility to Welsh crowds. Note the altered headlights, and extra road light. Cross-country rallys over rough terrain were very popular in Britain during the '30s and the fast Fords dominated there as they did in the U.S.

It doesn't seem right but sporty Fords were popular jumping objects at rodeos. A somewhat banged-up '32 Model B Ford *Roadster* takes its licks as the designated hurdle for a cowboy and his horse at a show in the mid-'30s. Folded windshield, and aftermarket wheels, give the car the lowest possible clearance, while a quilt protects against hoof prints.

Top right: In one of the top acts on the circuit, Cecil Cornish jumps his famous Brahma bull "Danger" over his '32 Ford V-8 *Phaeton* at an Oklahoma rodeo in 1940. Old Danger was trained to kick high above the sheetmetal but the repainted body of this now extremely valuable Ford model is a clue that he didn't always miss. Note the trailer hitch to pull the big bull. Also the luggage trunk for equipment.

Right: Like most Americans, the Depression was tough on travelling rodeo performers. But trick rider Billy Keen must have been doing OK. He is pictured making his famous "Standing Roman Jump" with a pair of trained horses over his pride-and-joy '32 Ford V-8 *Roadster* in the summer of 1933. Billy bought the Ford for its power to pull his horse trailer on the rodeo road.

THE 1933-34 FORD V-8S

Competition among automakers was keen in 1932. By now, Ford Motor Company had proven its speedy V-8 engine but it was clear that customers wanted cars with a better ride and more style. As a result, Edsel Ford developed the racy new Ford body styles for 1933-34 with rakish lines and forward opening "suicide doors." How this was accomplished with such relative ease is just another good example of his talent at turning a simple concept into a work of art.

It began at Ford's England operations where hard times in that country had created a demand for smaller and cheaper cars. The offices at Dagenham faced financial disaster unless it could come up quickly with a bantam unit to compete with the popular mini-cars — the Morris and Austin. Lord Percival Perry, head of the English branch, made a hasty appeal to the U.S. company for help and in October 1931, Henry Ford approved a plan to jointly engineer and style the new car at Dearborn.

Stylist Bob Gregorie was working on the next generation Lincolns when Edsel asked him to draw up the design for the "Baby Ford" which was to be designated the "Model Y". It had a 90-inch wheelbase with a tiny 8-hp 4-cylinder engine. According to Gregorie, "the job went along smoothly," and although it "was the car that got Ford of England back on its feet" he wasn't keen about its boxy appearance.

But Edsel saw something more in the lines of that little English Ford. To Gregorie's amazement he asked the young stylist to scale up the drawings of the dinky Model Y to fit the new '33-34 Dearborn Ford series. Explained Gregorie: "He just said, 'Look, take this car and step it up for 1933-34.' From there Kramer, the body draftsman (and) the body engineering department of Ford Company handled the whole process. They stepped it up a certain percentage (proportionally) . . . to produce the smart line for 1933-34.

I didn't realize it, till after the thing had gotten going that that was the order Edsel Ford had given to Engineering to do this. He didn't talk to me about it particularly. He was very pleased with the car, and he came to me one day and said, 'How do you like it?' I said, 'Fine.' He said, 'You recognize it?' I said, 'Yes.' "

"That's how Gregorie got started with Edsel," remarked engineer Gene Farkas, "He took him under his wing. . . . There was a lot of work done by Gregorie."

Credit for much of the final design work on the 1933 Ford models should also go to the company's main body supplier, Briggs Body Company in Detroit. Chief designer at Briggs at the time was Ralph Roberts who mostly designed LeBaron bodies in the custom division for Lincoln, and bodies for other clients such as Chrysler and Packard.

The way it worked in the early V-8 years was for Gregorie's approved designs to go first to the Ford body drafting room. Then, body supervisor Joe Galamb took them to Roberts' staff for further development into full-size wood or clay models. From there, after further improvements, the final plans went into production with some of the passenger bodies to be turned out by Ford, some by Briggs, and some by Murray Body Company; all with design input from Edsel, Gregorie, and Briggs.

With the new body designs came some new firsts in Ford engineering and science. One was a method of cranking the '33 side-window glass backward for ventilation. Another was the soybean-based "synthetic enamel" which would replace lacquer paint on Ford bodies that year. "This

Right: Edsel's classic '33 Ford design is one of the best examples of his extraordinary ability to create sensational cars during this time, without having the luxury of his own full styling department.

was also the first year that we conceded to put the same color on the fenders as we did on the bodies," recalled Ford chief engineer Larry Sheldrick. "This was really a step ahead. Prior to that, all our fenders had been black enamel, period. . . . Mr. Ford had always been insistent up to this point to have the fenders black. I think the change was brought about by sales demand, and Edsel's influence."

With a few small upgrades, Edsel's superb '33 models became the classy '34s. And it was fortunate that there weren't more changes because right in the middle of them Ford Motor Company was experiencing some of its darkest days.

The trouble came on the heels of the deepening Depression. With Ford sales plummeting, all the nation's banks were suddenly forced to close during the "Bank Holiday" of February 1933 — for awhile virtually ending all U.S. commerce. Then came the Briggs Body Company strike that drastically curtailed production and forced Henry Ford to take some strong action. "At the time of the Briggs strike," remembered Chief Engineer Larry Sheldrick, "the entire engineering force was laid off . . . with the exception of myself, Howard Simpson, Dale Roeder, and Ray Laird. When the Briggs strike was over he (Henry Ford) didn't open up the engineering department again. We had to coax him to bring back one man at a time."

Meanwhile, Bob Gregorie was one of the few men left in the body drafting department where he and Edsel worked on the few modifications to the new '34 model, such as the V-8 emblems, the double-handle hood design, and the grille changes. "The difference," observed Gregorie, "between the '33 and '34 . . . the bottom of the radiator grille on the '33 swept outwards, the '34 was perfectly straight — the '33 had curved louvres on the side of the hood panel, on the '34 they were straight." As usual, Gregorie would make a sketch. Edsel would then criticize it and make suggestions until they got it exactly right. Every detail was a refinement of his extreme good taste.

The result was a car so good looking that Gregorie bought one for himself and then customized it. "I acquired a '34 Roadster. They were pretty little cars — especially mine with some special touches. I had the boys down at the aircraft plant fix (it up) . . . It was really a beautiful thing. I had this special windshield and a special top, and I had some beautiful aluminum disc wheels turned for it."

Another interesting side note to this story is the Hupp Motor Car Company whose "Hupp Junior" sedan and cabriolet that year had '34 Ford body panels. It came about when Edsel approved a deal through Murray Body Corpo-

ration to allow the cash-strapped Hupp to use the sheet metal and some interior hardware. Edsel later turned down a similar request from Graham-Paige because their car was priced too competitively with the Ford.

(At the end of U.S. production, the 1934 Fords would take on a new life when all of the Model 40 Fordor Sedan body dies were sold to the Russian Government for use in their automobiles.) ◆

Fortunately, Edsel had a free hand in styling the '33-34 Ford V-8s without interference from his father who spent most of his time in the engineering department.

"... The development was in 1932 for a '33-34 series of U.S. Fords scaled up from my small English Ford design...." E. T. "BOB" GREGORIE, FORD CHIEF STYLIST

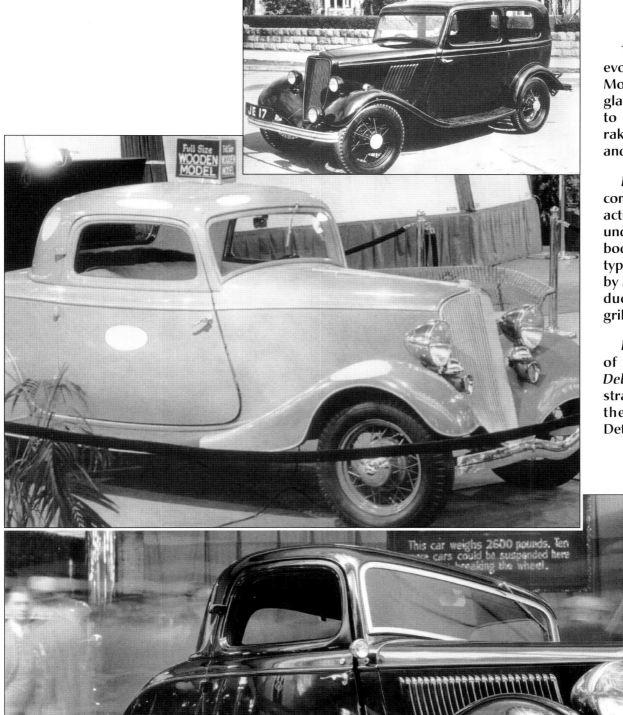

The 1933 Dearborn Fords evolved from Bob Gregorie's baby Model Y's designed for Ford of England. Edsel took the styling idea to a higher level, keying off the raked body lines, "suicide doors," and heart-shaped grille.

Left: Until Edsel got his own company studio in 1935, a lot of the actual Ford design work was done under his direction by the outside body companies. This wood prototype of the new *3-window Coupe* by Murray Corp. is nearly the production model but has an early grille concept.

Below: The production version of the beautifully executed 1933 *Deluxe 3-window Coupe* demonstrates the nimble ruggedness of the V-8 chassis at that year's Detroit Exposition of Progress.

Left: A worker polishes a sedan body on the line at Chicago. Ford chemists had just perfected a breakthrough new soybean oil enamel which would become standard on all Ford cars. It saved many hand operations in production and was more glossy and durable than lacquer.

Left: The first '33 bodies move down the Ford Chicago plant finishing line to receive upholstery trim, glass, hardware, instrument panel, and fabric roof insert. In the foreground is a *Deluxe 3-window Coupe* built-up from panels supplied by its contract designer, Murray Corporation of America. The Chicago plant had the ability to finish its own bodies from "knocked down" parts beginning in 1928.

Above: A 1933 Ford *Deluxe 5-window Coupe* is given final inspection at Chicago.

A finished '33 *Standard Fordor* body is lowered to a V-8 chassis at Chicago. The conservative *Standard* models came without cowl lights or chrome windshield frame, among other cost-saving features. The firewall on this car is also unpolished.

Right: It was a tough year for sales in 1933 and few plants in the auto industry were operating. At the slowed Ford operation in Chicago a rare close-up shows installation of one of the new 75-hp V-8 engines with cooler aluminum heads.

"The ignition system on the front end of the engine was a bad one. It cost the public untold millions in maintenance." LAURENCE SHELDRICK, FORD CHIEF ENGINEER

NEW FORD FOR 1933

The handsome new '33 Ford seemed longer but the wheelbase was still 112-inches — same as the '32 model. Here at Ford's huge Highland Park Plant showroom in Detroit a *Deluxe Tudor Sedan* gets measured to prove the point. Beyond the potted palm in the background can be seen a *Phaeton* model.

Left: Taking delivery of a brand new '33 *Victoria* at a Salt Lake City Ford dealer, May 27, 1933.

" . . . The (1932) V-8 introduction was a panic, that's about the only word suitable to describe that. From 1933 on it became somewhat more orderly . . ." LAURENCE SHELDRICK, FORD CHIEF ENGINEER

A steady stream of visitors viewed the new Ford V-8 112-inch wheelbase motor cars when they were put on display today.

The new Fords are the most powerful ever built. Fourteen body types are available, including both *Standard* and *Deluxe* types of the *Roadster, Phaeton, Coupe, Tudor* and *Fordor* sedans. The *Cabriolet* and *Victoria* are exclusive *Deluxe* types.

The new Ford bodies are characterized by a new and distinctively modern note, with flowing streamlines. The front-end ensemble of sloping Vee radiator grille, new skirted fenders, newly designed lamps, horn, and bumpers is most attractive. The windshield has a 20-degree slope. A wide choice of body colors is available. Colored wheels are optional on the *Deluxe* types.

Body interiors are exceptionally roomy, the bodies being materially wider and almost a foot longer than formerly. Seats are wide and deeply cushioned. Front seats in closed cars are adjustable. A choice of broadcloth, or mohair, upholstery is used on the *Standard* body types: *Broadcloth, Mohair* and *Bedford Cord* in the *Deluxe* models.

On all the *Deluxe* models a concealed ash receiver is located in the center of the instrument board, with a cigar lighter just above it. The *Deluxe Tudor* and *Fordor* sedans and Victorias are also provided with an ash tray in the rear compartment.

Safety glass is used in the windshield of all body types and in the rear windows of cars with rumble seats. *Deluxe* body types are fitted with safety glass throughout, while *Standard* body types may be similarly equipped upon special order.

All closed cars are fitted with dome lights while the *Deluxe* body types have cowl lights and rear compartment arm rests. The *Tudor* and *Fordor* sedans and *Victoria* have a convenient radio aerial. All *Deluxe* cars are equipped with twin matched horns, and two tail lights. *N. W. AYER & SON, JANUARY 31, 1933*

Just their kind of car. Mother and daughter see themselves riding in style in this sporty new '33 Ford *Deluxe 3-window Coupe* with the fashionable front-opening "suicide" doors. The enticing coupe, pictured at the Ford Highland Park show-room in Detroit, has the optional black fenders — a first for Ford this year. A '33 hallmark was the single hood latch.

Left: The cozy '33 *Deluxe* Ford driving compartment featured a combination horn-and-light-switch, an engine-turned panel holding the gauges, locking igni-tion, glove compartment, and handle to open the windshield.

Right: Hollywood's first female Oscar-winner, Janet Gaynor, shows off her new '33 Ford *Deluxe 3-win-dow Coupe.*

Ford men at the company's big High-land Park showroom check details of the new '33 *Deluxe Roadster*. These sporty soft tops came with *Genuine Leather* front seat cushions and a swing-up rear window that attached to a top bow to make it easier to communicate with rumble seat passengers. Special rod fittings and snaps on the doors were for stored side curtains that could be installed when needed to fully enclose the driving compartment.

FORD WINS ELGIN STOCK CAR RACE

Here's a story of Ford's V-8 performance that you cannot repeat too often.

It's the story of the road race of stock cars of 250 cubic-inch and under, held Saturday Morning, August 26th, at Elgin, Ill., under the auspices of the Elgin National Road Race Corporation and under the sanction and direction of the Contest Board of the American Automobile Association.

Fifteen stock cars were entered in the race – 11 Ford V-8s, 2 Chevrolets, 1 Plymouth and 1 Dodge, each driven by a licensed AAA driver.

The race was for a distance of 205 miles, 1,896 feet, over a course 8 miles, 2,499 feet long. The course included bad roads and concrete, tarvia, and gravel roads.

Fred Frame, nationally known driver and Indianapolis speedway champion, drove the winning Ford V-8, at an average speed for the race of 80.22 miles per hour, breaking the course record established in 1920 by Ralph DePalma. On one lap he passed the grandstand on the concrete at a speed of 100.3 miles per hour.

Of the cars that finished, the seven in the lead were all Ford V-8's. Frame was first with an average speed of 80.22 miles per hour. His elapsed time for the race was 2 hours, 32 minutes and 6.1 seconds.

This race afforded the opportunity for the Ford V-8 to meet its opposition on the open road, under the vigilant eyes of the country's highest automobile authority, and there it proved its all-around superiority beyond any question of a doubt. *FORD MOTOR COMPANY, DEARBORN, MICHIGAN, SEPTEMBER 1, 1933* _____

Fred Frame (extreme right) gets an official greeting during a Ford-sponsored cross country tour of cities to publicize Ford's big V-8 sweep of the 1933 Elgin Road Race. His wife sits behind the wheel of a roadster, which was actually a stand-in for the car that really won the race. That car didn't have chrome wheels or whitewalls, was a different color, and was lettered with its sponsor Cote Motor Company. It was on special exhibit through the summer and fall of that year, at the Detroit Industrial Exposition.

"... I think it was the idea of speed that led Mr. (Henry) Ford to the model V-8 ..." WILLIAM F. PIOCH, FORD ENGINEER

PRESIDENT'S SON DRIVES FORD V-8

Ford's advertising agency since 1927, N. W. Ayer & Son of Philadelphia, distributed this shot of FDR's son and his classy '33 *Deluxe Phaeton*. It has the rare optional side mount tires, equipped with fabric covers and dual mirrors. The wealthy Roosevelt's preferred to be seen in public with inexpensive cars. It helped their image with common folks during the Depression. Elliott's father had a series of Ford V-8 phaetons, equipped to drive with his crippled legs. His mother drove a Plymouth convertible.

Like many another man who loves the open air, James Roosevelt, Boston business man and son of the President, favors motor cars of the sport type. Mr. Roosevelt is pictured with his Ford V-8 *Deluxe Phaeton*. The top is down and the car is ready for a run through the New England countryside, now beautiful in the first warm days of spring. Mr. Roosevelt not only drives his Ford V-8 *Deluxe Phaeton* but also owns a Ford V-8 *Cabriolet*, which can be closed in when the weather is inclement. *N. W. Ayer & Son, April 27, 1934*

Sporting a brand new set of Vogue whitewalls and accessory 16-inch "artillery-spoke" wheels, a '33 *Deluxe Fordor* makes a pretty picture at a Hollywood studio in early 1934. Vogue Rubber Company's operations were at 24th Street and Indiana Avenue in Los Angeles. This firm was famous not only for its expensive sculptured whitewall tires but for its advertising billboards which were often platform backgrounds for real cars such as Vogue-equipped Auburns and Cords.

Opposite: Unintended, the simple beauty of Edsel Ford's 1933 Deluxe Ford V-8 design can be appreciated in this idyllic photo taken by a Pasadena, California, insurance company to record an accident that put a dent in the car's hood. Obviously proud of his fine-looking Ford, the owner had protected it the best he could with a pair of extra-tall accessory bumper guards. The wind-wings were also add-ons — good for driving on those hot summer days.

Low-pressure balloon tires or "air-wheels," offered by several U.S. manufacturers, had become quite popular on Ford V-8s by 1933. On smaller-diameter wheels with wider rims, and inflated to about 12 pounds, they gave higher speeds over rough roads. By far the most popular of these were the 14-inch General Jumbos, as shown installed on a 1933 Ford *Panel Delivery* belonging to the General Tire store in Salt Lake City.

Top right: Hollywood hero Johnny Weissmuller, 29, takes a break from swinging through the jungle while on location in 1934 filming "*Tarzan and His Mate.*" His choice of classy transportation to the set was this neat '33 Ford *Victoria* equipped with balloon tires and custom wheels, greyhound radiator cap, and windwings. Before making it big in the movies, Weissmuller was the world's best swimmer. In the course of the 1924 and

1928 Olympics, he won five gold medals, a record that was not equalled until 1968. He played Tarzan from 1932 to 1948 and later starred in the *Jungle Jim* series.

A couple with their new Ford *5-win-dow Coupe*, just equipped with snazzy General Jumbo white wall tires and 14-inch wheels, pause for a publicity shot at Jo Hall's tire shop in Tuscon, Arizona, in mid-1933. They can expect a much smoother, more floating ride. Note the modified tire cover to accommodate the balloon spare. The store's Standard *5-window Coupe* is at the left, with the more common cloth cover fitted over the spare.

NEW 1934 FORD CARS

The 1934 Fords were nicely upgraded from the '33s. A racy new *Deluxe 3-window Coupe* is pictured with other '34 V-8 models at a Houston, Texas, show. On a turntable at the left is one of the newly introduced *Victoria* models in attention-getting factory *Silver* show color, covered with glitter.

Left: Well supplied with dreams and sales literature, customers at Meier & Frank's department store in Portland, Oregon, get their first look at the new '34 Fords at a special showing. A noticeable change was the redesigned grille. The hotter new 85-hp engine — showcased in a cutaway chassis — would help make these the best-selling V-8s yet.

Important changes in engineering details and refinements in comfort and appearance features were revealed in the new Ford V-8 which was introduced this week.

Changes in the appearance of the car include new hood, radiator, and grille lines, a new instrument panel, and new upholstery treatment.

The body colors are to be used on the fenders of all *Deluxe* cars for 1934, and on Standard *Green* and *Gray* cars, with *Black* fenders optional. In addition to *Black*, the line of colors include a *Maroon*, a *Green*, a *Blue* and a *Gray*, with suitable complementary colors for wheels of *Deluxe* cars. Wheels on *Standard* models are *Black*.

Arm rests are provided on the doors of all *Deluxe* cars. New, more deeply cushioned individual bucket seats are provided for the driver and front passenger in the *Tudor Sedan*. Both seats tilt forward, and the driver's seat is adjustable.

Sun visors on *Deluxe* cars are new in style and so designed that they may be moved to the side, as well as lowered in front of the driver and side passenger. Operation of the door handles has been reversed. In the new models it is necessary to raise the handles to open the doors, which gives additional protection against inadvertent openings. *Ford Motor Company, December 9, 1933*

The photographer captures some great detail as a '34 *Cabriolet* body is swung onto a V-8 chassis at the Ford assembly plant at Louisville, Kentucky. The man in the foreground is at the position on the line where such delicate parts as hubcaps, headlights, and grilles are un–wrapped for installation.

Opposite: Workers at the Louisville plant trim freshly enameled '34 Ford *5-window Coupe* and *Pickup* bodies, along with other types, on a continuously moving line. At this section such parts as window regulators, glass, rubber, and top retainer, were installed before the bodies moved on to receive upholstery and then — further on to be mated with a chassis.

". . . At the end of another line the chassis starts. The motor is borne on still another line. The parts are joined — and, suddenly, there is an automobile. A puff of oil smoke snorts from its ex-haust pipe and it rolls from the line, ready for delivery." F. E. WYLIE, Louis-ville Herald Post, April 27, 1934

A pair of eye-catching publicity cars, provided by Ford for band leader Fred Waring and his "Pennsylvanians" during a week's engagement at Detroit's Michigan Theatre in August 1934, are pictured on a downtown street. At the top is a *Cabriolet* specially built at the Dearborn plant with demonstrator *Silver* paint — including the running boards — and accessory chrome-plated wheels. The *Deluxe Phaeton*, above, with its top stowed away neatly beneath the boot, was standard production — with just whitewalls and a greyhound radiator cap to enhance its natural beauty. Waring was under contract to broadcast the popular Ford Dealers radio show nationwide every Sunday night.

Cowboy movie star and former college football All-American, Johnny Mack Brown, poses with his sporty new '34 Ford *Cabriolet* at Lake Arrowhead Lodge in California. Purchased from Henry S. Perren, the dealer in Westwood, near Los Angeles, Brown's car has an accessory greyhound radiator ornament, and is equipped with a set of Kelsey-Hayes wheels mounted with classy Vogue whitewall tires. Kelsey-Hayes provided a good number of the 17-inch wire wheels used in '34 Ford production, which are distinguished from the regular Ford-made wheels by their bent spokes. Brown began his movie career in 1927, playing mostly in westerns. In 1934 he starred in "Belle of the Nineties."

GEORGIA PEACH QUEEN LIKES FORD V-8

Pictured is Miss Louise Efird, of Albany, Georgia, winner of the "Georgia Peach" contest at Radium Springs, and one of the finalists at the World's Fair in Chicago, with her Ford V-8 car. Miss Efird thinks it's "great fun" to drive a Ford V-8. "It has plenty of power and getaway, yet it is quite gentle and obedient, and I never tire of driving." *N. W. Ayer & Son, Ford Advertising*

"Miss Georgia Peach," with her new *Deluxe 3-window Coupe.*

Right: Window shoppers admire a stunning new 1934 Ford *Deluxe Roadster,* in the window of Paris Department Store in Salt Lake City, during a women's fashion promotion. The car's price, including the accessory bumperettes, greyhound radiator cap, and whitewall tires, was about $650.

Passengers board a Lewis Brothers '34 Ford V-8 bus at Salt Lake City. In these hard times a Ford was still the cheapest, most reliable transportation.

Right: Hopeful customers sign up for a drawing to win one of the new '34 Fords on display at Auerbach's Department Store in Salt Lake City. The cars, all *Standard* V-8s provided by local dealers to help stimulate business, included the *5-window Coupe* and sedan pictured. Another prize going to some lucky winner was a trip to the Chicago World's Fair, and a visit to Ford's Rotunda exhibition building as depicted by a scale model.

An evening crowd enjoys a Ford "Lawn Party" show in Salt Lake City, in July 1934. In the foreground is the new *Victoria* model with its novel canvas-covered tilt-back luggage compartment. It was Ford's only car with this design. In the background admirers ogle Ralph DePalma's speedy '34 Ford roadster dirt track racer that was on tour.

Left: A camping picture captures the back of a family's new '34 Ford *Victoria* with its luggage compartment open and the special snap-on canvas cover laid aside.

NEW VICTORIA ADDED TO V-8 LINE

The Ford V-8 *Victoria*, newest and smartest of the 1934 Ford body types, went on display during the past month.

Aside from its attractive streamline contours, which reflect the latest continental mode, the new *Victoria* presents two unique features, one a newly divided three-passenger front seat, and the other a large luggage compartment at the rear of the car.

Baggage or other articles may be carried in the luggage compartment with the compartment door closed, or, when occasion requires, the compartment may be left open to provide added space, and be protected with a canvas cover — which is provided. *Ford News Bureau, April 13, 1934*

Road racing great Ralph DePalma poses with his stripped-down '34 Ford roadster and a gang of admiring kids at the Ford Lawn Party in Salt Lake City. Born in Italy in 1893, DePalma migrated to the U.S., and in 1916 won the Indy 500. The legendary American driver usually wheeled Duesenbergs, Packards, and Millers but also had great success with the hot new Ford V-8s in the stock car events of 1933-34 — as did his famous nephew Peter DePaolo.

Louis Meyer's famous '34 Ford roadster at the Los Angeles Auto Show in 1935. Stripped boards and fenders, and cut-down windshield, were about all it took to make these speedy V-8s ready for the track.

"It took two years before Mr. (Henry) Ford was satisfied with the V-8 that was finally developed . . ." FRED THOMS, FORD ENGINEER

1934 OAKLAND STOCK CAR RACE

Battling for a cash prize of $1,500, Louis Meyer, a leading contender for the 500–mile sweepstakes at Indianapolis, took first place in a Ford V–8 in the 250–mile stock car race at the Oakland Speedway this afternoon from a field of 20 entries.

Sam Palmer, also driving a Ford V–8, took the second prize of $750, and also hung up the fastest time for a single mile lap of 81 miles per hour. Danny DePaolo, Ted Horn, Mel Kenealy, and Al Gordon, all in Ford V–8s, took the next four places in the event. Four other drivers finished in the money. Eight of the 20 entries were Fords, the other 12 being of four other makes.

Twelve thousand persons turned out for the race which was run on the Oakland banked-curve oval under a brilliant California sun. No accidents of any nature marred the event.

Throughout the grind, Meyer drove a steady cautious race. In the early laps the race appeared to go between Palmer and Gordon, but just after he had caught up with Palmer in the 108th lap Gordon lost time in the pits and Palmer streaked ahead. Soon afterward Meyer, who had been trailing up to this point, took the lead and never was headed. N. W. AYER & SON, OAKLAND, CALIFORNIA, MAY 6, 1934

What is it? Mechanics at the Monte Mansfield Ford dealership in Tuscon, Arizona, pose proudly with their custom '34 V-8. It's a masterful try at the famous '33 Pierce Arrow "Silver Arrow" prototype coupe design, and obviously a Ford from its grille to its wheels. Note the low silhouette, the airplane-type cockpit, the re-shaped fenders, the bullet headlights, and the "Vee" front bumper. Still, Edsel's stock '34s were pretty hard to beat for looks.

This wild-styled '34 Ford Official Car and hauler, with Brewster-style grille and bumpers, was a head-turner at the Mines Field dirt track in Los Angeles. It was part of the new Ford V-8 custom craze.

Below: The famous Brewster Body Company produced a number of stretched custom '34 Ford V-8s with daring heart-shaped grilles, winged fenders, and art-deco bumpers. One of the most unusual was this elegant convertible sedan model with artistic door and side-window treatment, and side mount spares. Specially built for McDonald Dodson, the colorful owner of Vogue Tire Company in Los Angeles, it naturally sports a set of his elite brand whitewalls.

Right: A fun '34 Ford *Roadster* getting full service at Tracy's Landing, Maryland, circa 1939.

Opposite: Looking for its first fare, a freshly two-toned '34 Ford *Fordor* Yellow Cab has its picture taken in Houston.

Below: A classic view of Pat Davis Ford, Houston, Texas, in November 1934. A service *Pickup* stands by while the lone new car for sale is a sporty '34 Ford *Roadster* equipped with General Jumbo balloon tires. The gas station with a Ford franchise was a Henry Ford experiment in the 1930s to foster competition but was so unpopular with the established dealers, Edsel prevailed on his father to drop the idea.

Edsel Ford and his design staff took great pride in their truck and commercial car styling. A fine example of their work is shown at the left on the salesfloor of Louisville Motors in Louisville, Kentucky, July 9, 1934. Pictured is a V-8 *Truck*, a 112-inch V-8 *Standard Panel Delivery*, a V-8 *Pickup*, and a *Sedan Delivery*, which has *Deluxe* car features except for painted horns and windshield frame.

Top: An outdoor showing of new '34 Ford commercial cars and trucks at Salt Lake City. Included are several truck models, a *Sedan Delivery*, a *Pickup*, a *Panel Delivery*, and a chrome-railed Service Body.

Top left: The *Salt Lake Telegram* found it newsworthy to take this picture of a Lux Soap traveling salesman with his handy '34 Ford *Sedan Delivery* at one of his grocery store stops.

THE 1935-36 FORD V-8S

By the time the '35 Ford model went on the drawing board in early 1934, automobile design began to be influenced by aerodynamics and the function of the chassis in providing more passenger comfort. Chassis engineer Gene Farkas told of how concerned they were at Dearborn that they didn't get run over by the competition. "Edsel Ford brought in the Chrysler Airflow and we went over that from one end to the other to see what the advantages were . . . I know (after that) we shifted the engine four inches forward."

This was the first time at Ford that the chassis engineers and body engineers were finally on the same page. They could all see the advantages of changing the frame and body mechanics for a lower center of gravity, lower seats and more room for the feet up front. Overall height was coming down and by making the bodies a little wider, you could squeeze in three people more easily across the seats. Instead of flying the fenders, the trend now like the Airflow was to close them in to help conceal the running gear and mud.

The Airflow wasn't the only influence on the '35 Ford design. Ford had its own futuristic car in the works – the Lincoln-Zephyr – being drawn up by John Tjaarda, head Ford stylist at Briggs. To keep the ideas coming, one of Tjaarda's men, Phil Wright, who designed the sensational Pierce-Arrow "Silver Arrow" was given the job to design the '35 Ford. This would be the last Ford model done purely by Briggs, from blueprints to clay models.

By now the Ford bodies had become even rounder and the use of compound surfaces in the fenders and rooflines had increased.

"Strange as it seems, we didn't work very far ahead (on styling) in those days," said Sheldrick. "We only worked less than a year ahead. Joe Galamb was sort of an advisor to Gregorie (who) carried the major responsibility . . . Gregorie's reporting directly to Edsel is an indication of Edsel's influence in styling."

As far as Henry Ford was concerned, styling still took a back seat to engineering. But if there was one thing the aging automaker knew about producing cars, it was how to read the sales numbers. His long-time body production man Joe Galamb knew the old man about as good as anyone and thought that in this area he was fairly predictable. "Mr. Ford always watched the sales," he said. "When the sales started to go down he thought either of cutting the price or changing the design a little bit."

So, the '35 Ford was cleverly face-lifted into the sleek all-new-looking '36 model by Holden "Bob" Koto, designer at Briggs Body Company. He made the sheet metal transformation from ideas dreamed up by Gregorie and from sketches Edsel liked of Tjaarda's Lincoln-Zephyr.

Gregorie's nautical background can be seen in the boat prow front-end of the new '36 Ford design, as well as the rounder, wider lines. Edsel's contribution as usual was the refinement of line, the trim details, fabrics, and colors.

A major new appearance feature of the '36 Fords was a new open wheel with wide-spaced lugs and a big 12-inch snap-on hubcap. "It was all for the reason to save weight," said Farkas, who worked on it. "Mr. Ford was great on reducing the unsprung weight as much as possible. . . . That meant scrapping about $5-million worth of wire wheel equipment, but even then, the saving was considerable. It was a much cheaper wheel to make."

Meanwhile, the bitter strike of 1933 by the Briggs Body Company had not set well with Henry Ford and he began taking steps to steer away from dependence on the outside body makers. At last he agreed with Edsel to establish a styling section within Ford to accomplish this goal. In early 1935, when the '36 Ford designs were coming off the

Right: **Some of Edsel Ford's small group of designers look over V-8 sketches at the company's first real styling studio in 1935.**

". . . During the thirties and forties, the whole thing was very simple, we just had a small staff, and Mr. (Edsel) Ford knew most of the boys in there by their first name, and it was all just a very friendly, folksy arrangement . . ." E. T. "BOB" GREGORIE, FORD CHIEF STYLIST

In the Ford styling department an early '35 V-8 sedan is pictured with an accessory luggage rack tried on for a rough fit and bracket adjustments. Other experiments and competitive cars for comparison are parked beyond.

Top right: Henry and Edsel Ford and production chief Charles Sorensen pose with the first 1935 Ford assembled at Dearborn. The senior Ford never understood the importance of good styling and gave Edsel little encouragement.

". . . I think the old gentleman had a feeling that Edsel Ford was too artistic for the automobile business . . . He (Henry) had established himself as a mechanical genius, so to speak. He didn't have any room for anything but the mechanics – the nuts and bolts . . ." E. T. "BOB" GREGORIE, FORD CHIEF STYLIST

boards, Bob Gregorie was promoted from body engineering to head of the Design Department. It was the first such organized department in Ford history.

Not everyone liked Gregorie. Joe Galamb felt slighted as soon as Edsel assigned certain projects to him and chief engineer Larry Sheldrick described Gregorie as "a very smart, cocky young fellow who knew it all and wouldn't take anything from anybody." "I would say Mr. (Henry) Ford didn't exactly like Mr. Gregorie," remembered engineer Emil Zoerlein. "He never had much to do with him. Gregorie's work was strictly with Edsel Ford and the rest of the management."

But Emmett O'Rear, who came to work for Gregorie in 1937, greatly admired him and thought he was extremely talented and ideally suited for the job. "He moved fast," recalled O'Rear in awe. "His brain was going a mile a minute. . . . He'd make a sketch and throw it over on a pile, and just go from one to another like that by the hour. His mind, apparently, was just literally on fire inside. . . . I'd never known anything like him before or since."

Gregorie was his own kind of character before he came to Ford and he didn't change his ways much through the years. He was a "very nice looking fellow" with red hair and a bright red mustache, slender build, and wore his clothes well. He had them made in London, and he wore knitted ties and colored shirts long before they became fashionable. He liked to wear his pants cuffs high, and sometimes showed up at work in the wintertime in a raccoon coat.

Tucker Madawick, another Ford stylist who came to work for Gregorie in 1937 said that on their first meeting he had, "a warm personality. He was a handsome man of Welsh, Scotch, and French. He wore beautiful Glenn Plaid suits, and he had buckskin suede shoes on, and wow!"

Gregorie's flamboyance now extended into marketing. One of the actions in his new role as head of design was to commission some catchy art to promote the sporty new '36 Fords through the company's ad agency, N. W. Ayer & Son. "So, I got Ross Cousins (as illustrator) and he was good," said Gregorie. "He could make nice drawings and show the car in front of a butcher shop, and a gal stepping out there and the guy putting the groceries in the back and all that kind of stuff."

There are some footnotes to the '36 Ford story. At the end of U.S. production some of the Model 68 body dies were sold to Briggs Manufacturing Company to be reworked into Ford of England's new Model 62s. Others, according to head of purchasing, A.M. Wibel ,were, "to some extent worked over into the Ford U.S. Model 78 (1937) requirements." ◆

"We would ask (clay modeler, Dick) Beniecki . . . What's the guiding principle here? And he sort of rolled his tongue around for awhile and mumbled, "Well, what you do is you put on what isn't enough and take off what's too much . . ."
EUGENE G. ADAMS, FORD STYLIST

Right and below: Assemblers at the Ford plant in Long Beach, California, in February 1935, attach fenders and jostle a V-8 engine into a chassis. Paper wrapped around the steering column protects the finish from the body which will be installed further down the line. Parts for this plant, which was located near Los Angeles, came mostly by Ford ship, via the Panama Canal, from the Rouge Plant in Dearborn.

Opposite: Plainly-equipped, but top-selling, '35 Standard Tudor Sedans come off the line at the big Twin Cities Ford assembly plant in St. Paul, Minnesota.

Beautifully equipped with the new 16-inch wheels in optional chrome-plate, one of the first '35 Ford Phaetons seen in Indianapolis was provided by Ford Motor Company for use of the 1936 Olympics horsemanship trials committee.

Top left: The clean lines of the new Ford *Deluxe Tudor Sedan* gets high marks at the New York Automobile Show January 12, 1935. It was the company's first appearance at this event in 25 years.

Left: On the stage of The Old Auditorium in Houston, Texas, together with promotional displays and a V-8 cutaway chassis, a racy-looking *Deluxe 3-window Coupe* and a pair of *Fordor* sedans are all set for a dealer presentation February 3, 1935.

FORD SHOWS 1935 MODEL

Marked by enthusiastic interest everywhere — and by the most complete presentation yet attempted by the company to usher in a new product — introduction of the new Ford V-8 car for 1935 was made to the country late in December.

The announcement program reached its climax when the new car was first displayed in dealer showrooms. Prior to this, fleet owners, independent garage operators, and service station attendants, were given previews of the cars in branches and dealer showrooms.

Most striking features of the new car are body lines which are distinctively modern and a definite departure from any previous Ford design.

The modern design note is carried without break from the new slanting vertical grille, with horizontal beading, through the sweeping line of the low hood, and more sharply slanting windshield, the beautifully moulded body, and the flowing rear quarter panel. Bodies are also materially wider. Fenders are of the body color, and deeper and more highly crowned, with sweeping skirts. Wheels are smaller, tires larger. The result is an impression of mass and stability most pleasing to the eye.

Slanting vertical louvres with horizontal stainless steel beading are combined to form an attractive hood-side ornament. The radiator ornament is fitted in position, the radiator filler cap being under the hood.

Upholstery and appointments harmonize with the remainder of the design.

Nine body types are listed. The following are available with DELUXE equipment: *Phaeton, Roadster, 3-window Coupe, 5-window Coupe, Cabriolet, Tudor Sedan, Fordor Sedan, Tudor Touring Sedan, Fordor Touring Sedan.* The *Roadster* and *Cabriolet* are fitted with rumble seats. FORD NEWS BUREAU, DECEMBER 1934 _____

1935 FORD CONVERTIBLE SEDAN

Record-setting aviator Amelia Earhart rides in the classy *Convertible Sedan* provided by Ford Motor Company to pace the 1935 Indy "500" race. This was the first Ford four-door convertible model, and the first with a fully collapsible top. The original prototype designed by Edsel's team had a rear-opening luggage compartment like the '34 *Victoria*, but the idea never developed and stowage was made behind the rear seat.

We have added a new type to our line of model 48 passenger cars — the *Convertible Sedan* — the price of which is $750.00 FOB Detroit. Shipments are expected to start from assembly plants within the next two weeks. We should reach a wide market through prospects desiring a smart, well built all-weather type car, particularly as we are the only company selling this style body in the low priced field.

This is a *Deluxe* type in every respect, including the chromium plated bars along the running board, the same as in the *Touring Sedan*. The back of the rear seat pulls forward to give access to the luggage space, and the upholstery will be in *Leather* or *Bedford Cord*, both of the same color and quality as used in the *Cabriolet*. Available body colors will be the same as those for *Deluxe* passenger cars. *GENERAL SALES DEPARTMENT, FORD MOTOR COMPANY, DEARBORN, MARCH 27, 1935*

Rust-prone, but beautiful, chrome-plated wire wheels were offered as fairly costly optional equipment through Ford dealers in both 1934, and 1935. A tantalizing '35 Ford 3-window Coupe is shown with a set of the fancy wheels at a Houston show.

TO OUR DEALERS

We are having an occasional call for Chrome-Plated Wheels for the Ford V-8.

In order that there may not be any delay when you have a customer who requests this type of wheel equipment, we will carry a few sets here, the price of which will be $17.00 per wheel and $85.00 per set of 5, subject to 25% discount to dealers.

While the quality of the chrome plating on the wheels is the best obtainable, on account of the varying road conditions, acids, salt spray, tar, gravel, etc., which might effect the plating of the wheels they must be sold without guarantee as to the permanence of the plating. *FORD, EDGEWATER, N.J., BRANCH, MAY 24, 1934*

Opposite and below: The zany Marx Brothers' comedy team of stage and screen clown with a new '35 Ford *Convertible Sedan* used to parade them through downtown Salt Lake City. They were in town for a one-week appearance at the Orpheum Theatre where their latest film "A Night at the Opera" was playing.

Right: The Marx brothers, left to right, Harpo, Groucho and Zeppo, cleverly disguised as regular businessmen, on their arrival at the train station in Salt Lake City. Their car is a conservative new '35 Ford *Deluxe Fordor Sedan* courtesy of the Ford district office for use during their engagement at the Orpheum.

Ford Motor Company attended the 1935 Indy "500" in a big way — not just underwriting Harry Miller's ten Ford V-8 powered race cars — but loaning all the official cars and trucks. A jaunty sport, properly attired for a man of his position, poses with a snazzy *Cabriolet* provided for AAA officials.

Top: In Southern California, Vogue whitewalls and chic aftermarket artillery-spoke wheels were all the rage. This pretty '35 Ford *Cabriolet,* parked outside a Hollywood movie studio, suggests a film star owner.

Few images of the 1930s capture the fun and excitement of the Ford V–8 — and the beauty of Edsel and Gregorie's styling work — better than this terrific publicity shot for Standard Oil Company by San Francisco photographer Charles Hiller. He was one of the best at composing his photos and, in this case, matches a pretty girl with a sporty new '35 Ford *Cabriolet* to promote the idea that it was his client who had the friendliest gas stations.

Neil McCafferty, of Los Angeles, was so smitten by the new '35 Ford that he designed a number of $1500 commuter airplanes around its styling, and speedy V-8 engine (turned backwards with the prop running off the crank). To make the point that it was '35 Ford-powered, he designed the plane's front to look just like a passenger model, and parked his dressed-up *Standard 5-window Coupe* alongside for a publicity shot to make the comparison. Note the car's neat after-market accessory disc wheel covers, and hood accent stripe.

Left: Service with a smile. A pretty delivery driver for a Detroit florist poses proudly with her new '35 Ford *Pickup.*

Below: By 1935, General had cornered the "changeover" low-pressure tire market. Sales slogans were "greater road protection," "added safety," "more comfort," and "smarter appearance." This '35 Ford *Pickup,* just equipped with a full set of 14-inch General Jumbos, including sidemount, is pictured at the Rand & Company tire shop in Berkeley, California. An outside display shows some of the store's other accessory wheel offerings — from wires to artillery spokes.

At the Houston, Texas, sales branch a new '35 Ford *Roadster* models the "high-wheels" soon to be offered to '36 Ford customers. An odd factory option that required special hubs, the spindly 18-inchers were for drivers who had to get through on any kind of road – and with this sporty soft-top, perhaps for oil company brass who wanted to ride the range in style.

Top: A veteran '35 Ford *Roadster* with stock 16-inch wheels for comparison.

FORD BUILDS "HIGH WHEELER" FOR DIFFICULT ROADS

A Ford V-8 *"High Wheeler"* for use in rural districts where exceptional road clearance is needed is now being produced by the Ford Motor Company. The car is equipped with 18-inch steel spoke wheels and 6:00 by 18 4-ply tires, instead of the 16-inch drawn steel wheels and 6.00 x 16 tires which are standard on the 1936 model. The additional road clearance enables the *"High Wheeler"* to negotiate roads with deep ruts and trails with high spots, such as stones and stumps. *N. W. Ayer & Son, January 27, 1936.*

Freshly delivered at Spokane, Washington, a 1935 Ford fire truck gets its picture taken before going into service. Hundreds of these were built for small volunteer departments across the nation. This open-cab type has the typical wrap-around grab rails, center-mount searchlight, hose reel, and ladders. The engine-driven pump is by Champion of W. S. & Darley Co., Chicago.

Top right: Modified from a regular '35 Ford sedan delivery, this smart-looking emergency car was built for Broussard's Ambulance Company in Houston, Texas. Pictured reporting for duty there at Hermann Hospital, it is nicely-equipped with aftermarket artillery-spoke wheels, including a side-mount spare sunk in the fender. The front passenger seat could be shoved forward to allow a stretcher.

Right: Mechanics at a Ford garage in Oklahoma City work on a '35 *5-window Coupe* patrol car. With the likes of Pretty Boy Floyd and Ma Barker and her gang still at large, state troopers needed the speed and agility of a tuned-up V-8 to give chase. The Ford's one shortcoming, for both the cops and robbers, were the old rod-operated mechanical brakes which Henry Ford refused to give up for better-stopping hydraulics.

L. BAILEY
PHOTO

FORD
LABORATORY

HIGHWAY
PATROL

STATE OF OKLA. DEPT. O

A comedy team of Los Angeles "Keystone Kops" checks out one of the city's new patrol cars – a 1936 *Standard Fordor Sedan*. The quick Ford V-8 would continue to be the top choice for lawmen nationwide.

Left: Rumble seats were on their way out. The new '36 Ford *Club Cabriolet*, which made its debut that spring with the rear seat enclosed, was the Ford convertible look of the future. The Ford front-end design went from flat to "boat prow" this year, influenced by Edsel Ford's interest in yachting.

"The changing of the models was left up to Edsel. He would come in and tell us each year what the model was going to be. He came in practically every day." JOE GALAMB, FORD BODY ENGINEER

NEW 1936 FORDS MAKE DEBUT

Ford V-8 cars for 1936 were shown for the first time today to Ford dealers at group meetings in Ford branches in 34 cities in the United States, and seven in Canada. The new units will be shown first to the public next Saturday.

Body lines will strike a note in conservative streamlining, a new treatment of the interior, and three important refinements in chassis engineering, summarize the principal improvements in the 1936 car. There are no radical changes. The 85-horsepower V-8 engine, of which more than 2-million are now on the road, is unaltered.

A new front-end treatment gives added distinction to the body lines. The hood is longer, extending gracefully over the attractive new radiator grille. With its vertical slots and more accentuated "vee", as well as its smoothly rounded lower edge which blends with the streamlined curve of the inner portion of the fenders, the new grille contributes a note of smartness which is distinctive and new.

Fenders are streamlined, a wide flare giving them an imposing appearance. Louvres are of new design. Horns are recessed in the fender aprons back of small round grilles beneath the streamlined headlamps. The latter are relatively small and parabolic in section, finished in enamel to match the body color, and set off by rustless steel rims.

The new steel wheels with 12 1/2-inch hubcaps materially improve the ensemble. Hubcap centers are of polished rustless steel.

Thirteen body types are available, ten with *Deluxe* appointments, and three without. These are:

DELUXE: *Three-window Coupe, Five-window Coupe, Roadster* with rumble seat, *Phaeton, Cabriolet* with rumble seat, *Convertible Sedan, Tudor Sedan, Fordor Sedan, Tudor Touring Sedan* and *Fordor Touring Sedan.*

WITHOUT DELUXE EQUIPMENT: *Five-window Coupe, Tudor* and *Fordor* sedans.
N. W. AYER & SON, OCTOBER 15, 1935

"That was Bud Adam's first job – to design the bands on the banjo steering wheels, the wires coming down to the center and back, held together by these clips . . ." JOHN NAJAAR, FORD STYLIST

Texas celebrated its Centennial in 1936 with a big exhibition at the State Fairgrounds in Dallas. Ford was there with its own popular pavilion, which included a tour to its nearby assembly plant where visitors could see how the cars of their dreams were made – like this affordable *Standard Tudor Sedan.* The Dallas plant also supplied cars and trucks for the Houston and Oklahoma City Ford sales districts.

Right: Texas assemblers muscle a V-8 engine into a chassis at the Dallas Ford plant in the summer of 1936. A tag on the steering column lists the build specifications for each car, such as body paint color, and options like the new Deluxe steel spoke ("banjo") steering wheel. Each Dallas-assembled Ford carried on its rear window a small sticker that read "Assembled in Texas by Texas Labor."

COUPE FAVORED FOR SPORTY PERSONAL USE

Short roof, long deck, round-top doors, and blind rear quarter, made the *3-window Deluxe Coupe* the sportiest and raciest of the '36 Ford closed passenger models. They especially appealed to women buyers.

Left: At Ford's Dallas, Texas, assembly plant a freshly-built Standard *5-window Coupe* leads a truck off the end of the line.

A favorite for spring and summer sports use is the Ford V-8 *3-window Deluxe Coupe.* Golf clubs, fishing equipment, and other sport paraphernalia are carried conveniently in the ample rear deck, accessible both through the rear deck hatch, and from the inside of the car, by raising the back seat. The rear window lowers, affording enjoyment of gentle breezes. Three can ride comfortably in the seat which is upholstered in a choice of *Mohair* or *Broadcloth.* The rear deck may be fitted with a comfortable rumble seat, available as special equipment. *N. W. AYER & SON, JULY 4, 1936*

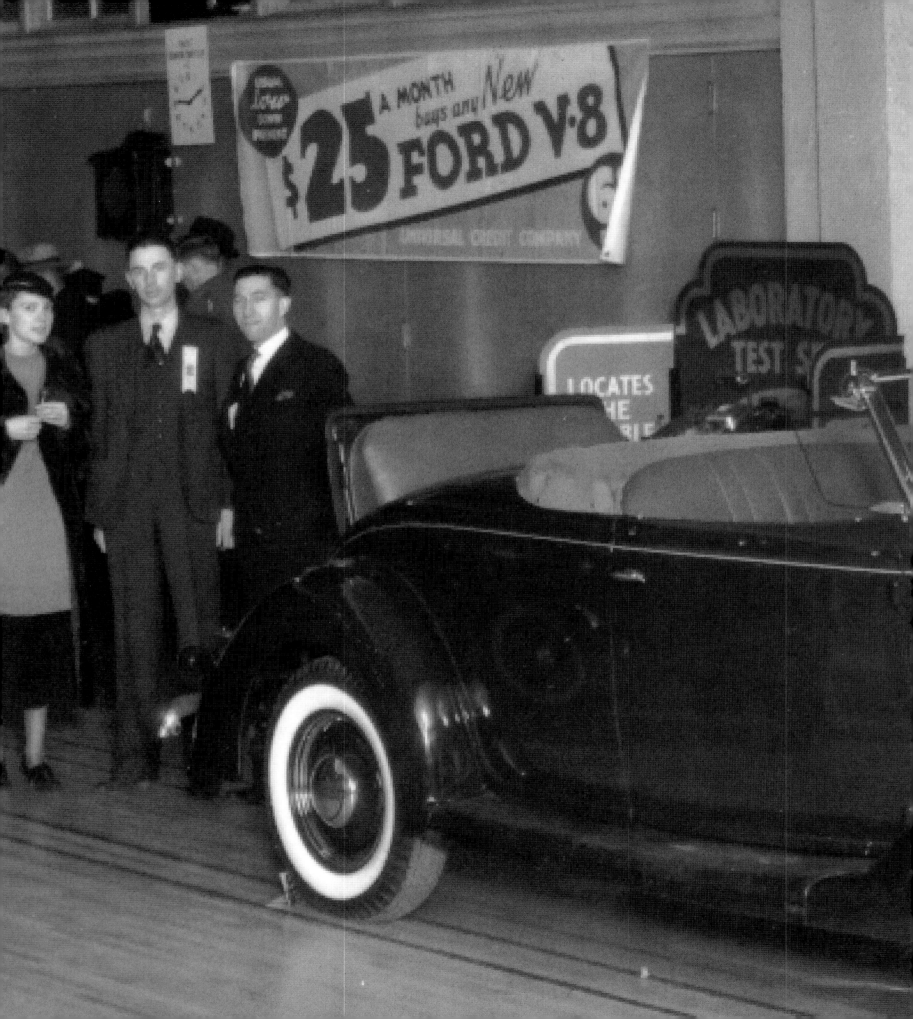

Through a peephole, a pretty girl and a saucy '36 Ford *Roadster*, called "The Car in the Clouds," wowed visitors to Ford's exhibition at the Atlantic City, New Jersey, Steel Pier during the summer of 1936.

Left: A close-up look at the new Ford V-8s at a Salt Lake City auditorium show March 1, 1936. Just a few dollars down and $25 a month would buy any car on the floor, including this breezy '36 Ford *Roadster*.

Below: A factory man explains the new '36 Ford 85-hp V-8 chassis, detailed in white show color, at a special "Exposition" showing of new models at a Salt Lake City dealer.

1936 FORD CLUB CABRIOLET

A new body type has been added to the passenger car line, to be known as the *Club Cabriolet*, the price of which is $675 FOB Detroit.

In exterior appearance it is very much like the *Cabriolet*, except that the top is slightly higher and extends back almost as far as the deck opening. It is in the interior, however, where a new treatment of *Cabriolet* design is to be found. Seat space is provided for five passengers, two in front and three in the rear, entrance to the back seat being accomplished by tilting the back of the front seat forward.

The car is *Deluxe* in all equipment with a choice of *Genuine Leather*, or *Bedford Cord*, for seat upholstery, and a choice of the usual *Deluxe* colors. FORD MOTOR COMPANY, GENERAL SALES DEPARTMENT, MARCH 19, 1936

An all-new Ford *Club Cabriolet* is an easy sale in the women's fashions section of Foley's Department Store in Houston, Texas. *Top right:* One of the sporty 2-seaters ready for a cozy ride at Dallas.

Right: The radiant winner of the 1936 Miss America pageant in Atlantic City, New Jersey, and a new '36 Ford *Cabriolet*, draw a crowd at Ford's summer exhibit at the Steel Pier. The regular single-seat soft top, with rumble seat and *Genuine Leather* seat cushions, was one of the two beautiful *Cabriolet* models offered that year.

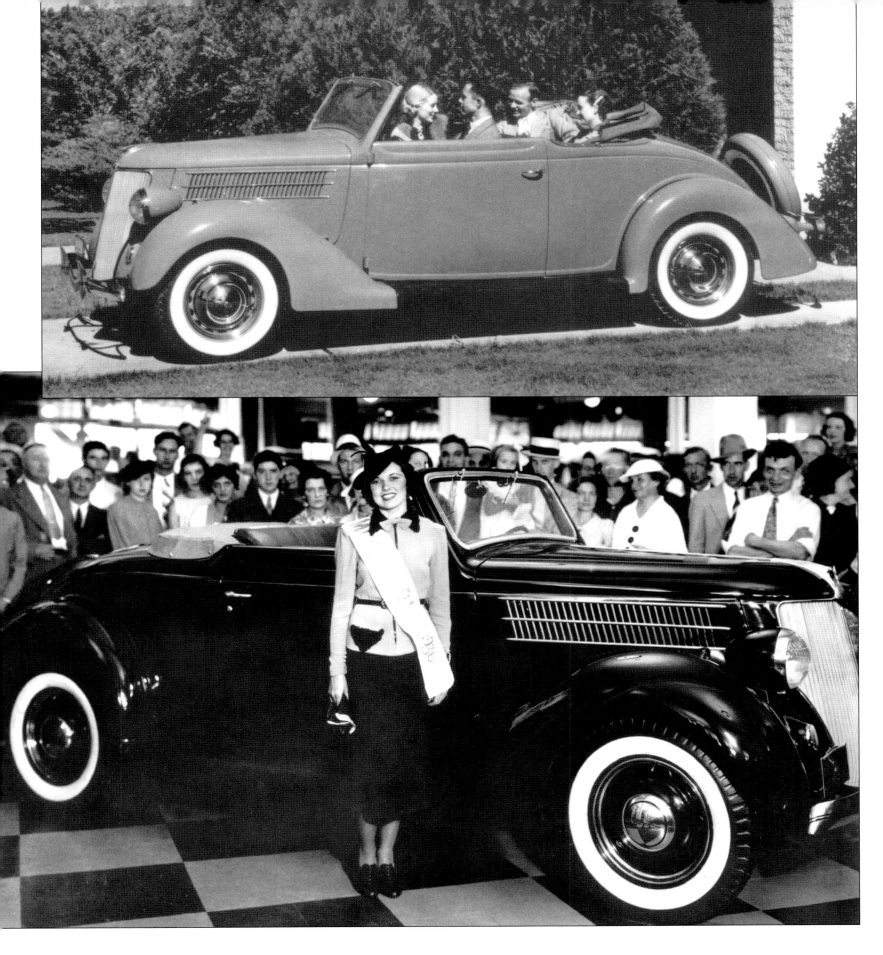

The Depression wore on. Sales were tough. Auto dealers still had to hustle to get their cars out to where the people were – such as the book section of Foley's Department Store in Houston. Here a salesman points out to a book shopper the features of a new '36 *Deluxe Fordor Touring Sedan. The* $650 price tag was plus shipping, and such extras as the deluxe wheel covers, dual wipers, and clock mirror installed on this car.

Top: A 1936 Ford *Sedan* is pictured equipped with some of the popular accessories offered that year, including sportlight, heater, and mirror clock.

1936 FORD CONVERTIBLE SEDAN

Making its debut at mid-year, the new '36 Ford *Convertible Sedan*, with a built-in trunk, was the first Ford passenger car to have a concealed spare. This one, fresh off the line at the Ford plant in Long Beach, California, is used to demonstrate the ease of stowing away luggage beneath the handier "clam-shell" deck design. The new configuration required unique stubby taillights, and license plate bracket carried on the deck lid.

The *Convertible Sedan* has been changed to incorporate a trunk and shipment of the new bodies to assembly plants started April 6th. The price of this new type is $780 list, F.O.B. Detroit, subject to the dealer's usual discount, all Federal and State taxes extra.

The trunk for this unit is of a different design than the one used on other types. Provision is made for carrying the spare wheel and tire on the inside, thus eliminating the use of a tire cover. An attachment on the lid holds it in an open position when desired, and it is so designed that a mere lift on the lid releases it when it is to be lowered. GENERAL SALES DEPARTMENT, FORD MOTOR COMPANY, DEARBORN, MICHIGAN APRIL 10, 1936

A *Deluxe Tudor,* one of the first 1936 Fords delivered at Salt Lake City, stars in a publicity shot with some sprightly co-eds on the campus of the University of Utah, October 31, 1935. The smoothly-styled "slant-back" Tudors were more for regular use than family travel since the only place for extra storage was a small compartment behind the rear seat.

Opposite: The ultimate '36 Ford V-8 shot! Beautifully composed for a Spring advertising layout by the Dick Whittington studios of Los Angeles are all the new passenger models — in Vee-formation — at the Long Beach, California, assembly plant. At the upper left, with black fronts, are the plain *Standard* types. Angled to the right, with chrome fronts, are the more expensive open and closed *Deluxe* cars. The entire lot at a dealer would bring about $9,000.

Stage lines and wealthy sportsmen found the Ford passenger car, with its strong frame, and powerful V-8 engine, an ideal vehicle to "stretch." This accessory-loaded 8-door "bus" was custom-built by a Chicago shop for Hollywood character actor Wallace Beery, who used it for hunting and fishing trips. There was plenty of room to take along friends, a streamlined carrier on top held all the baggage and camping gear, and the two extra seats inside folded into a bed.

Left: Several North American coach-builders produced 8-door stages in 1936 by stretching a regular Ford touring sedan. This excellent example was built for a New Brunswick, Nova Scotia, stage line. Note the all-weather clearance lights, dual wipers, and "V-8" insignia radiator winterfront.

Above: Star players of a 1936 youth league champion baseball team, sponsored by the Houston Ford sales branch, pose proudly in their Ford "script" uniforms.

Top: Baseball immortal, Babe Ruth, takes a close look at the milestone 3-millionth V-8, a 1936 *Deluxe Fordor Touring Sedan*, while on a visit to Ford's Rotunda showplace in Dearborn. After World War II, Ford Motor Company sponsored the slugger in a program to get more youth interested in sports.

A handsome '36 Ford 112-inch *Standard Panel Delivery* serves customers of a popular flower shop on San Jacinto Avenue in Houston, Texas. The nicely-signed two-tone paint scheme includes the radiator shell finished in the lighter upper body color, while an aftermarket greyhound radiator cap gives it some extra dash.

Opposite: Truck models, including a 1936 *Panel,* a *Dump Body,* and a *Cab-and-Chassis,* jockey for space at the busy driveaway yard of the Ford assembly plant in Richmond, California.

THE 1937-38 FORD V-8S

In his memoirs, Ford Chief Stylist, Bob Gregorie tells us that, surprisingly, the futuristic, so different-looking, tear-drop-shaped '37 Ford was really little more than a sheet metal makeover of the '36 model. "The '37 (Ford design) was taken from the first Zephr," he explained. "Briggs did that. Mr. (Edsel) Ford insisted they get something close to the first Zephyr. . . . The body was the same — the (1936) floor pan and roofline and all. So, it was just a front-end change. It was a face-lift deal. That's the last Ford that Briggs had anything to do with. After that, all that stuff was pulled out of Briggs and all handled in our department at Dearborn."

Gregorie's styling section at Ford was growing, anticipating the complete break with Briggs. Johnny Najaar, who apprenticed at the Henry Ford Trade School, was hired by Gregorie in 1937 and remembered what the design strategies were. "I know we all liked the idea of trying to get vehicles lower . . . to try to make body surfaces fit in a little bit better. . . . We thought we knew the future was to try to put headlights into fenders and ease up the surfaces, make the bumpers integral with the fenders, so they just didn't stick out there. . . . The windshield was angled aft with a purpose. . . . One was to reduce the inside reflections that you receive. . . . You could see your white shirt reflected in the windshield of the vehicle. It was hard to see through . . . and when they started to stamp these steel roofs . . . angling the windshield back at the top reduced the blank size of the sheet metal that they had to use to hit that area . . . (and) the running boards were . . . gradually reduced in width as the body got wider."

Emmett O'Rear also joined Ford Styling in 1937 and was astonished to find so few people in the design area. "There were only five men in the department at that time," he recalled. "Myself and Bud (Eugene) Adams were selected as top students from the Trade School, because Edsel Ford said, 'I think if we're going to build this thing up, we should try to do it with the young boys out of the school.' So they sent down there for two graduates, and Adams and I were selected . . . When I left four years later, they had 55 men, and that seemed a lot to us."

Adams' first job at Ford was to design the new deluxe "banjo" steering wheel.

Others working in Gregorie's department that year included metal fabricator Jimmy Lynch, "a master at doing propellers" from his days working in the Ford aircraft department; "pipe chomping" Dick Beniecki who was in charge of the clay modeling; and his assistant Bill Leverenz. Beniecki and Leverenz came from the disciplines of commercial sculpture, creating such works as the decor that went into Detroit's Fisher Theatre. Martin Rigitko, a big Austrian, was an outstanding body designer and the head draftsman. He came to Ford from Willoughby Custom Body Company and was much admired by the younger men. Bruno Kolt, from Germany, worked mainly on the grille detail.

"Nationality was a big item with Mr. (Henry) Ford," said engineer Fred Thoms. "A Swede is a good machine shop man. The Polish were good on production jobs. The Irish were good policemen, and so on. All the engineers were Hungarians. A French engineer is good, but they don't stick long enough. An Italian engineer is very good too, but they don't stay long enough. The English, Scotch, German, and Hungarians were the engineers. He preferred those men because they would stay."

The instrument panel designer was Johnny Walter, and the very talented Bob Thomas made sketches and worked on the clay models.

The wood shop pattern maker, John Hay, according to Johnny Najaar, "was a story by himself. . . . He came from Ohio and was quite a good craftsman. In order to get his job with Ford . . . he built a little model — a 4-door ('36 Ford) convertible model. It was about 12-13 inches long, and he made it out of tin cans, had them hammered together, soldered together, painted them. The model had full springing. The doors opened, the hood opened, the headlights lit, the tail lamp lit . . . and he sent that in. . . . When Mr. Gregorie saw that, he got Mr. Hay into our area right away."

Briggs Body Company styled the '37 Ford under Edsel and Gregorie's direction. Then the Ford body engineers coordinated the production.

As usual, Edsel never drew a line. His natural eye was so good he could create by merely criticizing an ongoing sketch or clay model. He would sit long hours in Bob Gregorie's studio, looking over his shoulder, making suggestions, until he had exactly what he wanted. "I'd never seen a sketch that Mr. Ford ever made," said Gregorie," and I presume that if he made them, he would have shown them to me at some point. . . . He never brought a sketch to me or ever took a pencil in his hand . . . but I knew he was intensely interested in artwork of every form. He was an excellent critic. By the same token, I would rarely ever suggest anything to him . . . to do something radical . . . and I have a feeling that he'd be offended if I suggested that sort of thing to him."

While the easy-going Gregorie thought the designs went smooth, the whole body transition to the '37 model in 1936 was considered by chief engineer Sheldrick to be "a real mess" because of the slowness of decisions on everything from body design to the body detail, trim, instrument panels and ornaments. Sheldrick was something of a "nervous Nellie" and got in the middle of one thing in his own engineering domain that nearly cost him his job. On the sly — out of sight of Henry — Edsel and production boss Charlie Sorensen had him working on an experimental chassis with hydraulic brakes. "They had a complete car made with side springs and hydraulic brakes, and everything," recalled Fred Thoms. "They brought Mr. (Henry) Ford over there, and he just looked at it and said, 'Get it out of here as fast as you can! Tear it down! Burn it up, or do something with it!' He didn't like it, because they did it without his knowledge."

Sheldrick survived that incident and from an entry in his engineering diary that year, he noted that the project to design the new 1938 Ford models began in March 1937. "We would have that design frozen by May or June. That would give them a few months to get the tools out," he said. "It was a mystery to me how we ever managed to work out a tooling program and a design change from March to the fall. I don't know how it was done but we did it."

The '38 Ford was the first completely designed within Ford Motor Company, and the first to be built in the new body plant at the big Rouge industrial complex in Dearborn. At last, Ford was free of the outside body makers.

It didn't come easy. In August 1937, while the body production facility was under construction at the Rouge, there was a sudden extreme shortage of body draftsmen. "The art of being a body draftsman," said Sheldrick, "is a profession all to its own. . . . A body draftsman is working with compound curves, working with three views, right on top of one another. . . . A body draft is made on an aluminum sheet, not on paper. The lines are drawn on the aluminum. It's very, very accurate work. . . . There was always a shortage of body draftsmen. . . . At this time, the shortage was caused by step-

ping up of yearly changes. . . . Body draftsmen were in demand by everybody. They were hijacking them, one company from another."

By now styling was seriously encroaching on Henry Ford's mechanical domain and Edsel had to be very diplomatic to make the case for his designers. As an engineer, Emil Zoerlein was often caught in the middle. "You have a peculiar split there." recalled the electrical system veteran, "which is true in almost any automotive company, between the stylists on one hand and the engineers on the other. Henry Ford represented the engineering side, and Edsel Ford represented the styling side. . . . "The stylist, of course, simply looked for looks while the engineer looked for efficiency. It was hard to convince Bob Gregorie that a little angle sticking out on the side cost you one-and-a-half horsepower at seventy miles an hour, and the equivalent in fuel."

True to his craft, Gregorie would always believe that customers didn't know a straddle-mounted axle pinion from a roller bearing, and didn't care. As far as he was concerned, they bought the car strictly on appearance. But Henry Ford was the boss and his side usually won any argument. "They (the stylists) were encroaching a little bit on the radiator," noted Sheldrick, "but it wasn't too serious. We could always get a cooling system in . . . The car that was planned for 1938 did bring the hood down so close to the radiator that the entire radiator had to be dropped. We were forced to put the fan down on the crankshaft instead of the normal position higher up. . . . The style dictated that and pushed it down there. In this instance, Edsel's idea won out over his father's. It was progress."

Even then, Sheldrick was often baffled by just how slow "progress" really was in his own engineering department. "You could never get a design crystallized out of Dearborn," he complained, "because the old man was monkeying with it (the chassis) all the time, . . . He monkeyed with it right up to the last minute, always changing his mind and never settling down. You could never get your tooling program worked in for production."

Bob Gregorie had sympathy for Sheldrick and his engineers. "They all saw the shortcomings of the old man's methods," he said, "It was too much of a rule-of-thumb system, too much edict engineering, and we were trying to do the engineering from facts rather than edicts. In other words, just because the old man said a thing would work was no reason that it was going to work."

It was an uphill battle. Henry Ford was nearing 75, but he was still boss. ◆

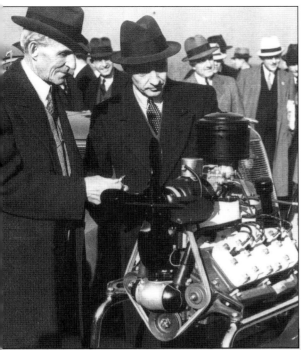

Henry and Edsel look over the new economy V-8 60 engine at the 1937 Ford press preview. The senior Ford thought people bought cars more for their engineering than styling.

Below: An early prototype front-end in clay shows the rudiments of styling that would evolve into the new 1938 Ford Standard model.

"... as far as I know Mr. (Henry) Ford never went down in the styling room. I never saw him in there. He didn't approve the finished style jobs ..." EUGENE FARKAS, FORD EXPERIMENTAL ENGINEER

THE MODERN NEW 1937 FORDS

A display of the new 1937 Ford models at Petty Motors in Salt Lake City, includes, from left to right, a *Deluxe 5-window Coupe, Fordor* and *Tudor* "slant-back" sedans, and a *Deluxe Sedan Delivery*.

Left: A group of dealers consider the sales prospects of the new radically-styled '37 Fords on display at a special preview held at the Louisville, Kentucky, assembly plant showroom. At the right is one of the stunning new Club Coupes.

The new Ford V-8 for 1937 goes on display tomorrow (Wednesday, November 11) at the Ford-Lincoln automobile show at the Hotel Astor, New York City.

The new car is the most beautiful Ford ever built. Its sleek lines flow without a break from the smart radiator grille, through the new shield-type hood, the new slanting V-type windshield, and the smoothly moulded steel top, to the graceful reverse curve of the rear quarter.

Virtually every visible component of the car reflects the "tear drop" form — the headlamps moulded into the front aprons, the highly crowned fenders, the chromium strips which border the hood louvres, the sweeping belt line, the arching curve of the top, and the finely formed rear body.

From a mechanical standpoint the most important development in the new Ford is the 60 horsepower V-8 "economy" engine, available besides the regular 85-horsepower V-8. The new engine is approximately two-thirds the size of the larger unit. Although new to America, it has been built in England and France for more than a year for Ford cars designed for the European market. The car's new brakes, designed by Ford to give "quiet" easy control, features a cable-and-conduit system for more controlled self-energizing action.

Eleven body types are available, including the new *Deluxe Club Coupe* seating five passengers. The new coupe is closely coupled, with an enclosed rear seat. The *Tudor, Fordor, Tudor Touring,* and *Fordor Touring* sedans and the *5-window Coupe* are available either with or without *Deluxe* fittings and with either engine size. The *Roadster, Phaeton, Club Coupe, Convertible Cabriolet, Club Cabriolet* and *Convertible Sedan* are *Deluxe* types, available only with the 85-horsepower engine.

The car's interior reveals a modern treatment. Upholstery is pillowed, with wide pleats. The instrument panel is grained, with the dials and engine controls in front of the driver. Starter button is on the dash, the hand brake at the left under the panel.

Six smart colors, including four which are new this year, are available. *Deluxe* cars will be available in all six colors. The two most popular colors, *Black* and *Washington Blue,* as well as a new color, *Gull Grey,* are available in both *Standard* and *Deluxe* types. The other three colors — *Bright Vineyard Green, Autumn Brown* and *Bright Coach Maroon* are available only in *Deluxe* types. FORD MOTOR COMPANY, DEARBORN, MICHIGAN, DECEMBER 10, 1936 ⸻

As a finished *Fordor Sedan* body moves by on a conveyor into the mammoth Rouge Plant in Dearborn, the nation's automotive press gets a preview of the new 1937 Ford models. Later, Ford dealers from across the country would come in by train for a sensational new model presentation at Detroit's Michigan State Fairgrounds.

Opposite: The *Tudor Sedan* was Ford's best-seller for 1937. Instructions slung on the front bumper of a *Deluxe* model being assembled at Dearborn tell what accessories, like whitewall tires, to install.

"... I would say that Edsel Ford had a tremendous amount of confidence in Gregorie and his ability and his decisions ..." *EMMETT O'REAR, FORD STYLIST*

The new '37 Ford V-8 was naturally pleasing to the eye. Bring out Los Angeles photographer Dick Whittington to compose the shot with a pretty blonde and even a staid "slant back" *Fordor* becomes a work of art. Edsel Ford and Bob

Gregorie might be amused to know that more than 60 years later Detroit was so hard-pressed for ideas that Daimler-Chrysler was driven to thinly re-working their design into the wildly successful, but woefully underpowered "PT Cruiser."

Engineering firsts for Ford on 1937 models included an all-steel top, split windshield, and an "alligator-type" hood opening *(right)*. In the photo below, the owner of a Gilmore gas station in Portland, Oregon, points out two more advances in the car's design that made it easier to service. One was the new gas filler location in the fender. The other was the handier location of the spare tire — now neatly concealed inside the flip-up deck lid of the newly-designed, built-in, rear luggage compartment.

Hardtop version of the *Club Cabriolet* was the sensational new 1937 Ford *Club Coupe*. With its rear seat and close-coupled lines, it offered a sporty ride without the bother of a drafty convertible top. This one is pictured at a show in Houston.

Left: A crowd mobs a '37 Ford *Club Coupe* at its debut at the Hotel Astor in New York City, November 11, 1936.

CLUB COUPE IS NEWEST FORD V-8 BODY TYPE

Newest of the eleven Ford V-8 body types for 1937 is the *Deluxe Club Coupe*, pictured here. Powered with the famous 85-horsepower V-8 engine, the new model is expected to have a wide acceptance among motor car owners. It is of the "close-coupled" type, with enclosed rear seat. The body has the compactness of the *Coupe*, while retaining the sleek lines of the sedan-type cars. The interior is surprisingly roomy. The rear seat is full-width. There is a roomy compartment under the rear deck, in which touring luggage may be stowed. *N. W. AYER & SON, DECEMBER 14, 1936*

1937 FORD ROADSTER

Top down, and rumble seat popped open, one of the rare (just 1,250 built) '37 Ford Roadsters is pictured (above and opposite) with other models at Carleson Ford in Salt Lake City, May 9, 1937. The low sales numbers of these sporty soft tops reflect a greater customer preference that year for either of two available types of all-weather Ford cabriolets with roll-up side windows, versus the *Roadster* with its drafty snap-on side curtains.

Top left: Another view of the Petty Motors showroom pictured on page 121, featuring a *Deluxe 5-window Coupe* with such accessories as whitewalls, *Deluxe* hubcaps, and dual wipers.

Sleek roadsters are as much a part of the springtime scene as robins and violets. The new 1937 Ford V-8 *Roadster* displays to advantage the sparkling streamlining of this year's Ford cars. This body type is available with deluxe equipment, and with the improved 85-horsepower engine. The wide seat, upholstered in antique-finished *Genuine Leather*, holds three persons. The seat back is split. Both sections may be folded down to reach the spare tire behind the driver's seat, and the rear compartment on the right. Rumble seat, and windshield wings are standard equipment. *N. W. Ayer & Son, March 1, 1937*

In its second year, the *Club Cabriolet* for 1937 was an Edsel Ford-directed styling masterpiece. With perfectly balanced proportions, extended top over a snug back seat, and fashionable buttoned upholstery in a choice of *Genuine Leather* or *Bedford Cord,* it was the ultimate fashion statement in Ford cars. Split front seat backs made access to the rear compartment easy. Still, given the nation's economy, the less-expensive two-seat model *(opposite)* outsold it.

A pilot and his sport plane at Los Angeles Airport comes up second best against the willowy young beauty's new '37 Ford *Cabriolet*. Today, she'd rather go for a drive.

NEW FORD V-8 DELUXE CABRIOLET

The new Ford V-8 *Deluxe Cabriolet*, pictured above, is one of the smartest of the 1937 convertible types. The full width seat accommodates three. Seat back is divided, the sections folding forward individually, to disclose the spare tire compartment back of the driver, or the luggage space opening on the right side. Rumble seat is standard equipment for the rear deck. The *Cabriolet* is available with the 85-horsepower engine. *N. W. AYER & SON, NOVEMBER 11, 1936*

FORD SHOWS SMART CONTINENTAL TYPE

One of the smartest of the new Ford V-8 cars is the *Convertible Sedan,* a continental body type which is becoming increasingly popular in the United States. It combines the advantages both of a closed and an open car. Its tailored top may be folded flat and covered by a neatly fitting boot. Safety glass windows in chromium frames may be lowered inside the doors. The interior is roomy, with seats and backs finished either in *Genuine Leather,* or *Cord.* Rear compartment fittings include foot rest and robe rail. Luggage may be stowed in the large compartment in the rear deck. The car is powered with the 85-horsepower V-8 engine. *N. W. Ayer & Son, February 20, 1937*

Dad, with his two boys, poses proudly with the family cars in front of their home in Oakland, California, in 1938. Alongside his pet Packard coupe is junior's sporty '37 Ford *Convertible Sedan,* made to impress his ivy-league friends with the addition of simulated Cord exhausts, which were the hot new dress-up items. Aftermarket front bumper guard, and accessory genuine Ford locking fender skirts, add to the custom look.

Nothin' to it! Awed cowboys in a '37 Ford *Convertible Sedan* watch Curly McCall make a no-hands bareback jump over their brand new car with his trained horse "Patches." It was at the JE Ranch rodeo in Waverly, New York.

One of the most famous western dude ranches of the '30s and '40s was the Pitchfork Ranch, about 30 miles south of Cody, Wyoming, outside the frontier town of Meeteetse. The author's grandmother was born here in 1895, where her father and his brother were cow hands. The huge ranch still operates today as a regular cattle outfit but during the Depression was opened to mostly wealthy eastern dudes eager to pay hard cash to enjoy a week or two among its scenic wonders, wear boots and big hats, and live among the cowboys.

In these photos, Cody pilot Bill Monday has just brought in a new load of customers with his trusty Ford *Tri-motor*. There to greet them on the ranch strip is the Pitchfork fleet of automobiles — all sporty jobs from the local Ford dealer in Cody. Pictured above is the Pitchfork's '36 Ford *Station Wagon*, and '37 *Cabriolet*. In the scene to the right, two more cars from the ranch are on hand for the welcome — a '35 Ford *Cabriolet*, and a new '37 Lincoln-Zephyr *Sedan*.

SLAYERS NABBED IN WILD AUTO CHASE

After the automobile dash that rivaled the melodrama of a typical motion picture bandit chase, two notorious gunmen were nabbed by Cass County, Nebraska, authorities as the climax of a nationwide man hunt.

The arresting officers, Sheriff Homer Sylvester (left) and his brother, Deputy Cass Sylvester, of Plattsmouth, Nebraska, attributed much of the success of the spectacular capture to their 1937 Ford V-8. In Sheriff Sylvester's own words:

"When my brother Cass wheeled my Ford V-8 out after those bandits that killed the G-man in Topeka, I knew we had them — because they didn't have a Ford V-8. They were hitting 60 or 65 when we picked them out by their Kansas license, but inside a mile and a half from a standing start we were right on their tail. Cass had the V-8 up to 85 right quick, while I looked after our guns and directed the chase.

"You can't fool me about automobiles — when I have to get somewhere sure and fast, the Ford V-8 is the only car for me. I've tried more expensive automobiles, but they couldn't do the things this 1937 Ford V-8 of mine will do any time I call on it. The 85-hp Ford V-8 is inexpensive to buy and cheap to run — and it's the best motor car I know of." *N. W. Ayer & Son, May 14, 1937*

Well-armed lawmen Homer, left, and Cass Sylvester, with their speedy '37 Ford *Fordor Sedan* which caught two armed bank robbers who were on the run after shooting their way out of an F.B.I trap, killing an officer. N. W. Ayer, Ford's Philadelphia advertising agency, was quick to get out a news release on the V-8's role in running down the gunmen.

Right: A new '37 Ford *Sedan Delivery* joins the British Columbia, Canada, Highway Patrol.

Below: Police in Vancouver, Canada, caught crooks with this innocent-looking cream-colored '37 Ford *Cabriolet.* Radio-equipped, with a hot V-8, it was ideal for the job. In 1934 infamous robber Clyde Barrow wrote Henry Ford about how much he liked the V-8's speed and how he, "drove Fords exclusively when I could get away with one." It didn't take cops long to figure out that it took a V-8 to catch a V-8.

TWO NEW FORD MODELS FOR 1938

Ford V-8 cars for 1938 continue the basic features which made them America's most widely chosen car last year — and in addition, provides a choice of two distinctly different lines of body designs. One line is known as the *Deluxe Ford V-8;* the other as the *Standard Ford V-8.*

The *Standard* car was designed for owners to whom economy in cost and operating expense is paramount. The *Deluxe* car provides added luxury and style.

A choice of two V-8 engine sizes is offered again for 1938 in three *Standard* body types. One choice is the 85-hp engine. The other is the 60-hp engine.

On the *Deluxe* models, the new style radiator is chromium plated, as is the windshield frame. Concealed behind the radiator grille are twin electric horns. Two windshield wipers, as well as two sun visors, are regular equipment along with front and rear bumpers and bumper guards, spare wheel, tire and tube, tire lock and band.

Deluxe car upholstery is in *Mohair* or *Broadcloth* tailored in new designs. Door and windshield moldings and the newly designed instrument panel are in a rich American walnut-grain finish. Seat cushions in convertible bodies are *Cord* or antique-finished Genuine Leather, while *Genuine Leather* is used exclusively in the *Phaeton.* Rumble seats are upholstered in waterproof artificial leather.

The eight *Deluxe* models are: *Fordor; Tudor; Coupe,* which seats three comfortably; *Convertible Club Coupe,* which seats extra passengers under cover of the sport top; *Convertible Sedan, Phaeton; Club Coupe,* which looks like a coupe but carries two or three in an extra seat; and the smart *Convertible Coupe.* All models have baked enamel finishes available in *Black, Blue, Brown, Green, Gray* and *Maroon.* Wheels and fenders are the same color as the body.

The three *Standard* models, the *Tudor* and *Fordor Sedans,* and the *Coupe,* are finished in enduring baked enamel available in *Black, Blue* or *Gray.* Fenders are the same color as the body, while wheels are black. Special colors on wheels and *Deluxe* colors on *Standard* body types are available at extra charge. FORD NEWS, NOVEMBER 1937

Mayor Smitley, of Tacoma, Washington, and his wife, admire a new '38 Ford *Standard 5-window Coupe* at Tommy Mallon Motors. For the first time, Ford buyers could choose from two distinct *Standard* or *Deluxe* price lines.

Right: Blossom time in sunny California is an opportunity to get a magazine cover shot of a pretty girl having fun in a brand-new '38 Ford *Convertible Coupe.*

FORD MODEL NUMBERS

Ford chief engineer Larry Sheldrick explained with some pride the mystery of how his Ford parts numbering system worked, beginning in 1938. ". . . It was a system wherein the model number would have some significance. The first numeral . . . indicated the year the model was going to be christened. The Mercury was to be a 1938 model, so the first numeral, '8', indicated 1938. The second numeral, '9', is a distinguishing label for the type of engine. Nine indicated the Mercury engine, the 239 cubic-inch engine. The 'A' indicated a passenger car . . . If that had been a truck, the last letter would have been a 'T'. If it had a European truck, it would have been a 'Y'. If it was a tractor, it would have been 'N'. The 221 cubic-inch engine, which was the Ford engine, was designated by the numeral '1', so the 1938 Model Ford car was 81A, and the 1938 truck (was) the '81T' or the '89T' — the '89T' because we used the Mercury engine."

RKO tap-dance starlet Ann Miller checks under the hood of a '38 Ford V-8. With her heart-shaped face, toothpaste smile, and long legs she was the cheerleader with the classy chassis and sequined tights who danced her way through twenty years of movie musicals. She made three movies in 1938 including "Room Service" with Lucille Ball and the Marx Brothers.

Proud Ford Motor Company of Canada executives outside their new Vancouver plant with a handsomely turned-out 1938 *Deluxe Tudor Sedan*.

Left: Assemblers build 1938 Fords at Vancouver. Cars and trucks were built on the same line here, at the rate of about 200 per week. Henry Ford's big Canadian subsidiary was headquartered across the river from company operations in Detroit, at Windsor, Ontario.

"... (in 1938) we couldn't exactly remedy the (brakes) or make the people forget the trouble we had in '37. They were good brakes up to a point, but they commenced to grab ..." *EUGENE FARKAS, FORD EXPERIMENTAL ENGINEER*

A view of the crowd at a showing of the new V-8s at the Ford Louisville, Kentucky, assembly plant May 25, 1938. In the foreground is a *Deluxe Convertible Sedan.*

Right: Hawk-eyed salesmen stand watch at a Louisville auditorium as visitors examine the new '38 Ford cars. Besides *Deluxe* or *Standard* models, and a V-8 60 or 85-hp engine, to choose from, *Deluxe* car buyers in March had a choice of two new Easter colors; *Dove Gray* or *Avon Blue.*

Top right: Edsel Ford is pictured at a company sales banquet in 1938. Admired by dealers, he was often at odds with his father's stubborn marketing ideas.

Teenage film sensation Judy Garland, soon to star in "The Wizard of Oz," tries out an open *Deluxe Phaeton* model while visiting Ford's Rotunda showplace in Dearborn with her mother March 25, 1938.

Below: A '38 Ford *Deluxe Convertible Sedan* on the salesfloor at a Louisville, Kentucky, dealer, makes a nice comparison with the car at the left. Note the different door treatment than that of the plainer *Phaeton,* with wind-up window handles and door top garnish mouldings.

A favorite prop, the popular Ford V-8s would play many leading roles in the movies. They were very photogenic, gave a great performance in speeding or taking a hairpin curve, and could handle almost any kind of abuse with ease — like this two-seat '38 Ford *Convertible Club Coupe* shown stealing another scene.

Below: A pair of brilliant white Ford Convertible Sedans furnished by local dealers for use of the Queen and her attendants during the annual 1938 Portland, Oregon, Rose Festival.

"... They (the engineers) had to realize that the design of the car was ... a hell of a lot more important than selling the customer as to whether the car had ... roller bearings or ball bearings in the wheels or what have you. They bought the car on appearance!" E. T. "BOB" GREGORIE, FORD CHIEF STYLIST

A Spokane, Washington, Ford dealer points out the fine engineering features of a new '38 Ford chassis, presented in cutaway detail and silver paint. The cars were plenty good looking but the old mechanical brakes were a tough sell when Chevy and Plymouth had hydraulics.

Right: Parts became art in the sales room of this medium-size Ford dealer in 1938. Steering wheels and V-8 symbols enliven the walls, fenders and grilles hang suspended from the ceiling, and accessories of all kinds, from hubcaps to mirrors, and radios, are mass-merchandised on counters. It was a setting that made shopping here a pleasure.

During the '30s Gilmore Oil Company, famous for its flamboyant promotional cars, planes, and economy runs, enjoyed a long business relationship with Ford. At the right, a '38 Ford *Deluxe Fordor Sedan* helps sportsmen find good fishing out west. In the photo below, another '38 *Fordor* is pictured cozied up for an advertising shot with a nifty Gilmore publicity plane at the Los Angeles airport.

Custom built for the rugged daily run to Nevada, some Lewis Bros. Ford V-8 passenger stages pose for posterity in front of the Utah Sate Capitol in Salt Lake City in April 1939. The pair on the left are '38 *Deluxe* models. The pair on the right are '37s — all on heavy-duty stretched chassis, with six-doors, roof baggage carrier, and side mount spare.

A photo from the Imperial War Museum in London shows one of the new '38 Ford "shooting brake" V-8 station wagons in service with the British Army that year. Built by Ford-England (note the cowl-mounted signal arms and fender parking lights), it is modified for North Africa desert campaigns with cut-out fenders to accommodate low-pressure 13-inch Dunlop balloon tires.

Right: The exhibit of cars and commercial vehicles at a 1938 Ford show at Vancouver, British Columbia, Canada.

EDSEL'S V-8 SPORTS CARS

dsel Ford enjoyed trying out styling ideas on his own personal Fords dating back to the Model T's when he was in his teens. When he became company president he drove custom Packards, and Lincolns, and was particularly fond of European sports cars. So, in the summer of 1932, with the idea that a sporty car along these lines might be developed for the American market, he decided to have his chief stylist Bob Gregorie design him one of those low-slung, two-seater, road racing types as an experiment. Years later, Gregorie vividly remembered the car: "Edsel Ford came to me and wanted a special body built on one of the first '32 V-8 chassis, and I drew up a little boat tail speedster with cycle fenders — a pretty little thing. We had it built partially in the Engineering Laboratory and over at the Lincoln plant. . . . It was gunmetal gray, gray leather upholstery, and so on. . . . "We had a fellow named Rosie, and he was an expert metal beater. He'd beat those fenders out on a big leather bag filled with shot. . . . He'd beat hour after hour, and he'd shape that metal around into the most beautiful shapes by hand. . . . Robinson — "Robbie" we used to call him — was the manager of the (Lincoln) plant. Robbie and I and two or three of the maintenance men there did most of the

work on the car. When the car was finished (in the fall), Mr. (Edsel) Ford made the comment that it cost $25 to drive a nail there in the plant at that time. He said, 'You should see the bill I got for this car.' Of course it was all Ford money."

Gregorie told of how they kept the project well away from Henry Ford, who never would have approved. But it was a way Edsel could keep good men working who otherwise would have been laid off during the Depression. "I think he felt good about keeping a few people busy, really . . ." As for the neat-looking little European-style '32 Ford V-8 boat tail sports car, Gregorie recalled that Edsel took it home, used it a lot ,and then it disappeared.

Edsel had little time for custom roadsters in 1933 because of serious company problems related to the continuing Depression. But, when the situation brightened the next year he had a new idea for a sports car. It was the summer of 1934. The previous June, one of that year's economic casualties was the Ford Tri-motor airplane, which ceased production after a total of 196 were built. It was Henry Ford's only try at commercial aviation, and, as able and popular as the venerable "Tin Goose" was, it was never profitable. The shutdown left the Ford aircraft plant in Dearborn with just a skeleton crew of sheet metal workers and eight or ten top mechanics to provide parts and service for the old Tri-motors. These were some of the most skilled men at Ford and to make sure they didn't lose them

Left: **Edsel Ford and Bob Gregorie dreamed up a series of low-slung V-8 sports cars in the 30s. Here, Gregorie takes the neat '34 job for a spin.**

for lack of something to do, Edsel put them to work doing experimental work for his top stylist Bob Gregorie. It was a place Gregorie could work on Edsel's special projects away from his regular Ford activities — and "the old man."

"That summer," said Gregorie, "discussions about a Ford sports car came up again. (So) I developed a sports car chassis based on the 1934 Ford. All that we used from the '34 Ford was the chassis . . . the power unit and so on. I developed a special front-end suspension which enabled us to lower the car down five or six inches and also to extend the wheelbase about ten inches. . . . Later, the two front fenders were made from Ford Tri-motor fenders — the aluminum stampings, which covered the wheels on the Ford Tri-motor landing gear. . . . So we finished the car up . . . and I sent it over to the Lincoln plant, had some nice trim put on it, and had it painted — Mr. Ford's favorite gunmetal gray."

Gregorie also remembered building a '35-type Ford sports car for Edsel the following year. "Along about February 1935, we talked about putting it into production through one of the custom body builders. . . . We'd furnish the chassis, the custom body builder would provide the bodywork and finish it up, and it would be sponsored by Ford. Well, anyway (nothing developed from that idea). Mr. Ford gave me the car which I enjoyed very much having. . . . I used it for a couple of years . . . made several trips down east with it — a beautiful car . . . I sold it for $500 and don't know what happened to it."

There were probably at least two good reasons why the '35 Ford sports roadster built by Gregorie never got beyond the prototype stage. One was the failure that Memorial Day of any of the ten Ford-financed Miller front-wheel drive V-8 race cars to finish the Indianapolis 500 (an expensive Edsel project that peeved his father). The other was that Edsel had found another outlet for his sports car idea.

After the Indy races, in the summer of 1935, Edsel was visiting England and made some business agreements with Jensen Motors Ltd., at West Bromwich, a company that made sports cars. "They (already) used certain Ford components" said Gregorie, ". . . Ford engines and whatnot . . . So we made an arrangement with them to use the chassis — this particular chassis design that I developed." The Ford stylist noted that his design didn't change anything mechanically except that it lowered the car down — lengthened the wheelbase ten inches and gave a better ride, nicer handling. "Beautiful suspension for a sports car. We built two more hand built chassis, crated them up,

and shipped them from the Lincoln plant to England. He (Edsel) sold them on the idea, and the conversion parts were made in the Dagenham Ford plant." Jensen designed and built the bodies for these cars with 1936 U.S Ford-style fronts and used Gregorie's chassis. According to him, "on a few hundred a year" until production stopped in 1939 for the duration of the War.

The 1936 Jensen-bodied Ford sports cars were particularly handsome. Hollywood businessman Percy Morgan imported two of then to the U.S. Interviewed in 1971 by this writer, the dapper Morgan said his cars were equipped with the regular U.S. V-8 chassis (modified by Jensen), which he shipped over to beat expensive English import duties on the Gregorie-type. One of the cars was silver. Morgan's friend, film star Clark Gable, ordered this one on the condition that he liked it when it arrived. He ended up opting for a Duesenberg instead, and the car was sold to another party. The other '36 Ford-Jensen was black and Morgan kept it for 23 years, driving it flamboyantly around Hollywood and his country estate in Montecito, California. Both of these cars survive in the hands of collectors.

Edsel and Gregorie were always dreaming up ideas for cars. The gifted Ford stylist had nothing but the highest regard for his boss. "Oh, terrific. What a man. We had some of the greatest discussions — if I wanted to build a special-built car of some kind. . . ." One of these was a custom '38 Ford *Landau Sedan*. "I took a Ford two-door, and I blanked out . . . the rear quarter window, sent it over to the Lincoln plant, and had it filled in and paneled with landau leather like on the custom-built Lincolns, and it was all trimmed with pigskin. It was a beautiful thing, and I had a special paint job put on it at the Lincoln plant. I had told him (Edsel) what I had in mind — showed him a little sketch of it. He said, 'Well, we have to do those things to find out, don't we?' . . . So he drove it home one night, and he said, 'Gee that's nice and quiet, rides nice with all that padding in the roof.' He always liked the idea of a special-built, custom version of a Ford . . . see? The basic Ford, but let's do something to it to make it a little different."

Edsel's work with Gregorie on these projects would ultimately climax with one of the greatest automotive design achievements of the time — the famous award-winning 1940 Lincoln Continental — fashioned by Gregorie from the uni-body V-16 Zephyr. Before this terrific idea came along, the pair had been seriously thinking about making a marketable special sports car out of the Mercury. ◆

Ford 4 onder de kap.

Edsel Ford wanted to market a European-type sports car something like the racy-looking '37 Matford-Alsace Cabriolet pictured above, produced by the company's own Ford-France. With his chief sylist, Bob Gregorie, a series of experimental Ford V-8 roadsters were built — leading to the production of the car he really wanted — the Zephyr-based 1940 Lincoln Continental.

Bottom: From a regular production tudor, stylist Bob Gregorie designed this custom '38 Ford *Landau Sedan* for Edsel in their quest for a sporty V-8 that was marketable.

12-22-37   /28/ FPO

MICHIGAN 1932
271·747

"... I drew up the sections of it like you draw the hull of a boat and developed the panelling for it and so on ..."
E. T. "BOB" GREGORIE, FORD CHIEF STYLIST

Edsel always liked European sports cars. The fast new '32 V-8 chassis gave him a chance to experiment so he had Bob Gregorie design and build this wild boattail speedster. It was one of the first Ford concept cars ever — and one project the senior Mr. Ford didn't know about.

Right: The very first '32 Ford hotrod! Edsel's fully custom V-8 speedster was dropped, had cycle fenders, a re-worked boat-prow grille, racy windshield, and bullet headlights. It was used as a personal car around his estate.

Bob Gregorie's second Ford V-8 sports car, built for Edsel's personal use was this speedy Buggatti-like gunmetal gray roadster, pictured in the summer of 1934. The low-slung car was doorless, had a boattail rear, a heart-shaped grille, fared-in driving lights, and front fenders bor-rowed from a Ford Tri-motor airplane. The front-end showed a hint of boat prow-shape — a good indication of Edsel and Gregorie's thinking, leading to the '36 Ford designs. This car has survived and now belongs to a Florida collector.

"I know that Mr. E. T. Gregorie did a number of roadsters for Edsel prior to the time the (styling) department was formed, and at that time keeping the wheels separate from the body, doing a little race car..." JOHN NAJAAR, FORD STYLIST

160

Bob Gregorie, top left, is pictured with another of the V-8 sports car experimentals he designed for Edsel Ford in 1935. Looking much like the later British MG, with its cut-down doors, stock grille shell, and deep hood sides, it had a convertible top, a flat rear section, and "flying" front fenders. Disc hubcaps covered the wire wheels. Gregorie said the main idea with this car was to sell the sports chassis in some volume to custom body builders. Nothing came of it, so Edsel gave him the car.

162

According to Gregorie, Edsel sold some of his Ford V-8 sports car chassis to Jensen of England who added their own bodywork. This superb silver '36 Jensen was imported by Hollywood businessman Percy Morgan for actor Clark Gable, who decided not to buy the car. It is pictured at the left with film actress Faith Domergue, and above with her father Leo Domergue, sales manager for Ham Nerney Ford in Hollywood.

Above: Leo Domergue admires the specially-fitted V-8 engine compartment of the 1936 English-built Jensen-Ford. The cars' design was based on earlier ones by Bob Gregorie, and featured an all-aluminum body with "suicide" doors, folding windshield, leather upholstery, and Lucas lights. A set of accessory "deluxe" Ford hubcaps and Vogue whitewalls completed the "Hollywood" look.

THE FORD SHOW COLORS

*F*ord often produced vehicles that can't be documented by records. One of the most exotic examples is the flashy series of show cars that were specially painted by the company in light colors never found in the sales literature. Among early V-8s, they would have to rank high among the most desirable ever built.

Edsel Ford specified these cars. He was particularly fond of *White* or light-*Cream* colors, because he felt that nothing showed off the lines of a car better. But, as all the other automakers learned in those hard Depression times, light-colored cars just didn't sell. Americans only wanted dark colors. (This would stand in sharp contrast to the happier postwar boom years when, by 1960, the top-selling color for all Fords from Falcons to Lincolns, was *White*.)

So, in 1933, to continually test the market for changes in the public taste, Edsel specified that cars in the light colors could be ordered by dealers as "demomonstrators." He expected these light-colored cars to liven up new car introductions and other publicity events. His plan was that they would be specially painted by a prearranged factory scheme, used as demonstrators, and eventually sold to daring customers.

Typically, these eye-catching V-8s would be finished in the Ford commercial paint department. With the "Special Paint Request", which had been used mostly by truck buyers since Model A days (and is still available today), cars could be routinely ordered at extra cost, from a large stock of colors in almost any combination. For fleet operators, popular colors such as *Vermillion Red* were always available, along with greens, blues, and many shades of cream. Among the known promotional colors used from time to time were *White*, which dated back to the '26 Model T; *Silver*, starting with the '31 Model A; and *Demonstrator Yellow*, specified for '36 Ford commercial cars and trucks. It was no problem to factory paint a car in just about any color the customer wanted, so long as he was willing to pay the extra $25 or so for the special job.

Ford kept few records of these operations, so just what colors were specified for the special-order show cars can only be assumed from an occasional clue. A Factory and General Offices Letter #216 dated January 5, 1935, from Ford Dearborn to the Buffalo, New York, assembly plant. states in part that "it is specified that *M-2822 Ford Vermillion Red* and *M-2842 Ford Medium Cream*, in two-tone diagonal body scheme is the special 1935 Ford commercial car and truck demonstrator color." This was the main color scheme for the Ford promotional fleet provided for that year's running of the Indy "500," and may explain one shade of cream for early V-8 demonstrator cars. Other possibilities are *M-938* and *M-1224 Tacoma Cream*, popular colors for wheels and body striping, and *M-1742 Cream*, used on trucks and commercial cars.

The color *White*, which became the official color for Ford show cars from about 1937 — and V-8 cutaway chassis even earlier — is easy enough to identify. It has always been a regular commercial listing. But even Ed Spagnola, the respected COLOR-ITE paint supplier of Bethany, Connecticut, who helped with this story and has been researching Ford paint for three decades, has never found a formula for *Ford White*. The assumption is that it was considered such a standard color that Ford didn't feel it had to be explained.

So, with little more than the pictures to document them, here's a close-up look at some of those truly outstanding *Cream* and *White* show cars — to prove they were available to the public, and in a class of famous Ford V-8s all by themselves. ◆

Right: Among the least known early Ford V-8s are the factory-production "demonstrator" or "show" cars. National speedway champ, and twice Indy "500" winner, Louis Meyer is pictured with one of them — a *cream* and *Vermillion Red* Ford *Deluxe 5-window Coupe* — at the Indianapolis track in 1935. Part of the fleet of publicity cars provided by Ford Motor Company for that year's Memorial Day Race, it is painted in the typical demonstrator theme with *cream* bumper brackets, and horns.

Light-colored cars found few buyers and were rare during the Depression. So, Ford used them to attract attention — like this stunning new cream-colored demonstrator model '34 *Victoria*, pictured at a public Open House held on the lawn of the Louisville, Kentucky, assembly plant.

Below: A glamorous '33 *Victoria* factory demonstrator, specially finished in a shade of cream with a coating of glitter, revolves on a turntable at a Ford tent exhibition in Houston. After such use, these show cars would go to customers.

At a special Meier & Frank department store introduction of the new '34 Ford models at Portland, Oregon, a sexy *Cabriolet*, in cream "demonstrator" color with contrasting wheels, awaits the crowd.

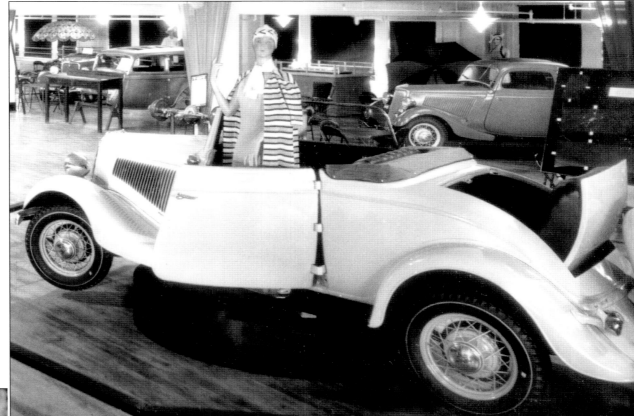

Below: In one of the the most glamorous early Ford V-8 photos ever, Hollywood film star Joan Crawford shows off her gorgeous '34 Ford *Roadster* which was specially ordered for her from the Long Beach plant in cream show color. Her car not only has the telltale factory cream bumper brackets, etc., — but a cream-colored steering wheel! Her dealer added the perfect complimenting accessories — from custom wheels with Vogue tires, to greyhound radiator cap, dual spots, and roadlamps.

By 1937 the specified color for Ford "show cars" had progressed from shades of cream, to pure *White* — like this dazzling, side-curtained '37 *Phaeton* for the Queen of the Portland, Oregon, Rose Festival.

Left: A *White* '40 Ford *Convertible Club Coupe* was part of the spectacular show which ran daily at the company's New York World's Fair exposition building.

Below: Photos of cars carrying the reigning beauties in the 1937-48 Portland Rose Festival — like this rare '40 Mercury *Convertible Sedan* — have provided a lot of what is known about the *White* Ford show cars.

THE '39-40 FORD-MERCURYS

The big issue in the development of the '39 Ford model was hydraulic brakes. All of his competition had them. Henry Ford hated them! His national sales manager, the popular John R. Davis, had a particularly tough job trying to sell customers on the old Ford steel brake system, lamenting, "Henry Ford was reluctant to accept progress that represented the ingenuity of someone else — in fact any adaptation from Chevrolet or Plymouth was absolutely taboo." Davis also had to defend the Ford's old rougher-riding buggy-style transverse springs, when all the other automakers had gone to the modern semi-elliptical type.

Engineer Fred Thoms put the brake situation in plain terms. . . "Mr. Ford objected to the hydraulic brake because it wasn't his brake. He hadn't developed it."

"God knows Edsel tried to get hydraulic brakes put on the car," said stylist Bob Gregorie, "and a suitable suspension system, and other improvements which were far past incorporating in the product."

It was the sales figures that, as always, finally convinced the old automaker that he could no longer postpone the change. But he was so upset about hydraulic brakes that he wouldn't drive them for the entire year they came out, afraid, according to him, that, "If that liquid for some reason or other gets low or you lose it, you'll have no brakes." So, he drove around with the old '38 brakes on his new '39 Ford.

Tucker P. Madawick joined the Ford styling department in 1937 and was a bit confused by, on the one hand, Henry Ford's resistance to change — and Bob Gregorie's class operation. But, being new, Madawick steered away from any styling controversies with the engineers, saying, "It didn't make any difference to me, because I had a '35 Ford *Phaeton* then, and that was the greatest machine. It was something! I drove it to Dearborn without side curtains; didn't need side curtains then. If it snowed, you put newspapers on the seat, and you'd shake the newspapers out . . . The one I had had two inches of concrete poured in the back between the seats right on the floor with the tunnel for the drive shaft. They needed weight back there. So I had it." As

for the job. "We knew that Ford was different then than General Motors and Chrysler. They were three distinct automobile personalities . . . General Motors was number one, and we were number two, and Chrysler was number three. . . . I would say the environment was good. It was tops. And we were growing then. . . . We had some new, fresh cars emerging. We (at Ford) had the best. We had absolutely the best in clay. We had the best in ovens, we had the best in (styling) bridges."

Automobile styling came so easily to Gregorie that he was almost apologetic that his great Ford designs, like the '39 model weren't better. "I think the little Fords we did," he said, "considering most of them were just face-lift jobs in '39, '40 . . . I mean, we were very limited in what we could do. None of those cars was a straight out — from the ground-up design — the old body section, the body shell went back years . . . it was just a matter of front end mostly."

Emmet O'Rear remembered helping style the '39 Ford. "An awful lot of the real design was done right on the clay, like the taillights and a lot of the ornamentation. Gregorie would sit there with a knife and carve away on what we were working on, and he just went from one place to another."

One of Gregorie's men was Bruno Kolt, formerly a sculptor, who worked in clay and wax. "They used him a lot on the lettering," said O'Rear. "It's the first time I'd ever heard that on 'Ford' the 'O' always needs to be a little bit larger than the 'F' and the 'R'. If you made them exactly the same height, it would appear to be smaller because of the trick of the eye. . . . He always said to trust the eye. Don't trust measurements, trust the eye."

By the time the 1940 models were on the drawing board, events had reached the point where the company was

Right: At the 1939 New York World's Fair, newsmen and spectators crowd in for a look at Henry and Edsel Ford with their milestone 27-Millionth car — a Ford *Deluxe Tudor* — just arrived on a highly-publicized tour from the west coast where it was built at the Richmond, California, plant.

moving along without as much interference from its founder Henry Ford. Charles Sorensen pretty well had his way in production; A.M. Wibel in purchasing; Larry Sheldrick in engineering; and Edsel running the business. In 1938, at age 75, his father had suffered a mild stroke and was slowing down. But he still came by nearly every day to tinker in the engineering department. Otherwise, he appeared somewhat lost.

"He came in to my Design Department," said Bob Gregorie, who had learned not to show him anything until it was nearly complete, "and he'd look around, and I'd just start to describe something to him . . . He'd throw up his hands, and he'd say, 'That's between you and Edsel. That's between you and Edsel.' . . . That's all he'd say. Then he'd walk out." Gregorie did remember very clearly that during this time Mr. Ford still had enough fight in him to resist all suggestions of putting independent suspension under his cars. But he did give in to a combination torsion bar and sway bar stabilizer for the '40 Ford front suspension that was needed because of the softer springs, which were added for a better ride.

In his memoirs, Edsel's longtime secretary A. J. Lepine described the younger Ford's daily routine during this time. "Mr. Ford would come to the office about 9:30 and then leave about 1:00 for the round table (staff lunch at the Engineering Laboratory). I think the procedure here was, after lunch, for the executives (Edsel, Sorensen, Weibel, etc.) to accompany Mr. Henry Ford around the laboratory, stop here and there, and discuss mechanical subjects that might have been of interest. . . . I presume that somewhere about 4:00 or 5:00 p.m. might be Mr. Edsel Ford's leaving time. (He) had a complete command, in my estimation, of the commercial operations of the company. He knew about sales and advertising. He frequently had discussions with the chief purchasing agent, and he got reports from the factory about production, manpower and that sort of thing. . . . He also had an unusual insight as to production and engineering as applied to the car. . . . It was simply my opinion that he had a good grasp on everything."

"He was also very critical about the quality of the automobile as a whole," said engineer Emil Zoerlein. "For that reason he asked us to take cars off the production line at will . . . tear them down if we liked, look them over and show them to him."

Edsel was always trying to push the Ford cars to a higher level of quality and, as they were soon to be judged in the marketplace, his handsome 1940 models came closest yet to hitting the mark. ◆

Henry and Edsel Ford discuss the merits of the new sealed beam headlights which would be incorporated in their new 1940 models.

Henry Ford checks a calculation with experimental engineer Emil Zoerlein who developed the V-8 ignition system he wanted — and always regretted the trouble it caused.

An early clay model concept shows some of the evolution that led to the final design of the 1939 Deluxe Ford front-end. Note the screw jack holding up the heavy form, the small hood-side V-8 emblem in the rough, and the prototype Mercury body at the right.

Inset above: Prototype bumper accessories, and grille paint scheme, are tried on a nearly finalized '40 Ford Standard model.

"By 1939, when we were preparing for the 1940 model, we were giving ourselves a little more lead time than we had in previous years. We were pretty well started very early in 1939 for the 1940 job . . ." E. T. "BOB" GREGORIE, FORD CHIEF STYLIST

". . . I can remember back then, "Taiilight Bill" Wagner sitting at the back of . . . the first Mercury — there was like a tin can-like thing for a taillight mounted on the side of the fender, and he would model that taillight himself, and then take it very carefully from the right fender and lead it over to the left fender so it would work. And, that is true for the headlamp doors which were built into the fender — anything that could be moved from the right hand to the left hand was done. And that was because they only needed one tool . . ."
JOHN NAJAAR, FORD STYLING

Craftsmen test engraving rolls for the wood-graining operation on the new '39 Ford instrument panel. The hand manipulated soft rubber wheels explain the mysterious technique in which the beautiful mahogany wood effect was applied to every curve and crease, even the inside of cut-outs like the glove compartment door.

Right: Stylists freeze for a publicity still at their studio inside the Ford Engineering Building at Dearborn March 23, 1939. In progress are some of the coming 1940 Ford passenger car and truck, models. The mobile clay modeling bridge (extreme right) was used to look down to ensure that the car's contour line flowed smoothly from the front hood line and top to the rear quarter panel.

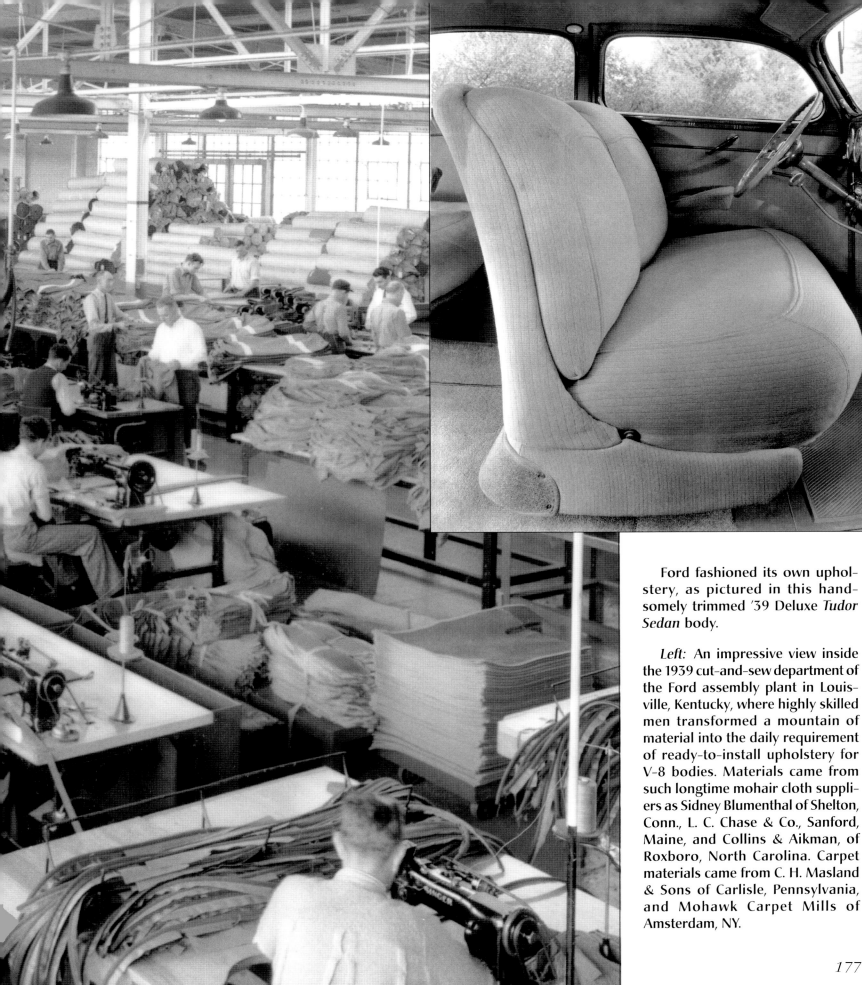

Ford fashioned its own upholstery, as pictured in this handsomely trimmed '39 Deluxe *Tudor Sedan* body.

Left: An impressive view inside the 1939 cut-and-sew department of the Ford assembly plant in Louisville, Kentucky, where highly skilled men transformed a mountain of material into the daily requirement of ready-to-install upholstery for V-8 bodies. Materials came from such longtime mohair cloth suppliers as Sidney Blumenthal of Shelton, Conn., L. C. Chase & Co., Sanford, Maine, and Collins & Aikman, of Roxboro, North Carolina. Carpet materials came from C. H. Masland & Sons of Carlisle, Pennsylvania, and Mohawk Carpet Mills of Amsterdam, NY.

177

NEW 1939 FORDS DEBUT

Introduction night of the new 1939 Ford line at Petty Ford in Salt Lake City, November 5, 1938. Left to right is a Ford *Deluxe 5-window Coupe*, and a regular Ford V-8 *Standard Fordor* with its distinctive front-end styling.

Left: On the same evening pictured above, as a band plays and best friends pose for the camera, a new '39 Ford *Deluxe 5-window Coupe* is admired at the crowded showroom of Raymond Pearson Ford in Houston.

The two finest Ford cars in the 35 years of the company's history will be given their first public showing tomorrow (Friday, November 4) in dealerships throughout the country. The cars are the 1939 *Ford V-8* and the 1939 *Deluxe Ford V-8*. They are individually styled. Both are of compelling beauty. Both have hydraulic brakes.

The *Deluxe Ford V-8*, with wholly new streamlines, has a distinctive appearance of its own. At the same time, both it and the *Ford V-8* share a family likeness with the Lincoln-Zephyr and the new Mercury 8.

The *Deluxe* has a deep hood with long lines unbroken by louvres, low radiator grille in bright metal, and wide-spaced headlamps set into the fenders. The words *Ford Deluxe*, in script letters of chrome are divided at the front of the hood. The hood handle is concealed in a vertical extension of the radiator ornament.

The 1939 *Deluxe* is powered by an 85-horsepower V-8 engine of even more rugged construction than the 5,000,000 already in use. The *Ford V-8* is offered with the same engine as the *Deluxe*, or with the economy 60-horsepower V-8 engine.

The *Ford V-8* for 1939 has a full grille and unobtrusive louvres at the rear of the hood lines. Headlamps are recessed into the fenders. Decorative touches include a radiator grille ornament which incorporates a compact hood latch and handle.

All body types have large luggage compartments. In fact, the coupes in both lines have two luggage compartments and large shelves for parcels as well. Driver seats are adjustable in all body types. All are equipped with sun visors, and dual windshield wipers with a single control. There are dual electric horns on the *Ford V-8*, and twin electric air horns on the *Deluxe*.

The *Deluxe Ford V-8* is available in seven attractive colors. There are five body types: *Tudor* and *Fordor* sedans, *Coupe*, *Convertible Sedan* and *Convertible Coupe*. The *Ford V-8* is available with three color options and in three body types, *Tudor* and *Fordor* sedans, and *Coupe*. N. W. Ayer & Son, Inc., November 3, 1938 ⎯⎯⎯⎯⎯⎯⎯⎯⎯⎯⎯⎯

The '39 *Convertible Coupe* was Ford's last car with a rumble seat. A popular new spring color offered in May of that year for *Standard* and *Deluxe* Fords was *Cloud Mist Gray*, replacing *Gull Gray*.

Left: A handsomely presented '39 *Deluxe Fordor* on display at Temple Square Hotel in Salt Lake City.

Top left: A *Deluxe Tudor* arrives by truck for exhibit in the lobby of the Paramount Theatre in Portland, Oregon.

1939 DELUXE FORD V-8 CONVERTIBLE COUPE

This smart *Convertible Coupe* typifies the modern appearance of the new *Deluxe* Ford V-8 cars. Influence of Lincoln-Zephyr styling is apparent in the low radiator grille, long hood, and streamlined body. The interior is cozy. Seat cushion, and backs, are in *Russet Genuine Leather*. Tops are *Tan-Gray*, or *Black*.

Brakes are hydraulic, engine 85-horsepower, body all-steel. Equipment includes twin air electric horns, dual windshield wipers, and sun visors, headlight beam control, battery condition indicator, cigar lighter, ash tray, and locking glove compartment. Rumble seat is standard. Luggage is carried in rear deck, or back of seat. *N. W. AYER & SON, OCTOBER 28, 1938*

Newsmen interview Edsel Ford about the new car models at the company's exposition building at the 1939 New York World's Fair.

"I don't think Mr. (Edsel) Ford had any taste for random publicity ... There was a disposition on his part to avoid the excess publicity of people who think it desirable to be in the public eye ..." A. J. LEPINE, EDSEL FORD'S PERSONAL SECRETARY

The huge Fort Peck federal dam project on the Missouri River at Fort Peck, Montana, created a boom-town with lots of workers with money to spend. Looking for sales, the Ford branch in Fargo, North Dakota, set up this exhibit in the town's big government auditorium. On display is the full line of 1939 Fords, Mercurys, and Lincoln-Zephyrs, ranging from sedans and convertibles, to trucks and commercial cars.

Left: Ford road man Gordon Peterson, from the Fargo Branch, lectures a Ft. Peck crowd on the V-8 chassis, and the new hydraulic brake system.

"... The Mercury, there really wasn't much to it ... It was a variation of the Ford. A little more pleasing body lines, and as far as we were concerned, it was just a blown-up Ford in many respects. Mr. Ford (Edsel) had insisted on the car being called the 'Ford-Mercury' — hubcaps, battery, window glass stenciled. ... That didn't read right to me because we were trying to sell the car to an income bracket above the Ford. That's why the DeSoto was created. That's why the Pontiac was created.

"I said, 'Mr. Ford, I have second thoughts about having the name Ford-Mercury on the car.' 'What do you mean?' he said. 'What's wrong with the name Ford? Isn't it good enough for this automobile?' That was the only time I'd ever seen him flare up at me. I told Mr. Ford, 'You know, you turn the ignition on in this car, and it sounds like a Ford, the exhaust sounds like it, the whole thing. And, not only that, but the competition says, get down and look under the car ... If that isn't a Ford — radius rods, buggy springs. . . . Well, anyway the following week down at the New York Auto Show, the sales managers and branch managers, climbed all over Mr. Ford. He was down there. In the meantime, I had my boys get together racks of hubcaps without the Ford name on them. (When Edsel got back from the show) there was never a word said after that. We just changed it over to the Mercury hubcap, and they got the Ford name off." E. T. "BOB" GREGORIE, FORD CHIEF STYLIST

1940 FORDS SHOWN

The *Ford V-8* and *Deluxe V-8* cars for 1940 present notable advances in styling, comfort, convenience, and safety.

Body lines are pleasingly streamlined, but not extreme. Front-end designs are distinctively modern, with low radiator grilles; long, well-proportioned hoods, and deeply rounded fenders. The trimly tailored interiors are big and roomy, with plenty of seat room, leg room, elbow room, and shoulder room.

The design of this year's *Deluxe Ford V-8* establishes the car more firmly than ever as a style leader in its price class. There are twenty-two important new features on the car, including finger-tip gearshift on the steering post, controlled ventilation, and Sealed-Beam Headlamps for safer night driving.

The 1940 *Deluxe Ford* is powered by the 85-horsepower Ford V-type 8-cylinder engine – pioneered in the low-priced field by Ford nine years ago. The Ford V-8 engine, first in a stock car setting below $2,000, has been so enthusiastically accepted by the motoring public that to date some 6,000,000 are on the road.

Five distinctive body types, including a new *Convertible Club Coupe*, comprise the 1940 *Deluxe* Ford line. Other models are the *Fordor Sedan*, the *Tudor Sedan*, the *Coupe* and the *Business Coupe*.

In the *Deluxe* line there is a choice of six body colors: *Black, Cloud Mist Gray, Folkestone Gray, Lyon Blue, Yosemite Green* and *Mandarin Maroon*.

Careful color harmony and fine tailoring distinguish the interior of the *Deluxe Ford V-8*. Windows and door frames are finished in *Dark Mahogany;* handles are *Maroon*. Knobs and escutcheon plates are plastic in a rich color. Upholstery is a pleasing new sand shade – available either in striped *Mohair* or fine quality *Broadcloth*. Seat cushions in the new *Convertible Club Coupe* are *Saddle Brown Leather*.

On the handsome instrument panel, all gages are grouped in a single unit for perfect visibility through the new two-spoke steering wheel. There are two ash trays, one at each end; a lighter; grille for a Ford radio speaker; a thirty hour clock, and a sturdy lock on the glove compartment. *FORD NEWS, OCTOBER 1939* _____

The beautifully styled 1940 Fords were well received by a public feeling good about a general upswing in the nation's economy. Pictured in the foreground left to right at the Detroit Auto Show October 24, 1939, is the new *Standard Business Coupe, Deluxe Tudor Sedan*, and *Deluxe Coupe*.

Right: A plain but attractive 1940 Ford *Standard Tudor Sedan* stands ready for budget-conscious buyers in a Detroit showroom. The front-end design, much like the '39 model with painted trim, was clearly distinct from that of the *Deluxe* car.

1940 FORD V-8 DELUXE COUPE

The new *Deluxe Ford V-8 Coupe* for 1940 is unusually roomy. Three can ride on the seat in perfect comfort. A new finger-tip gearshift is located on the steering column. This clears the front compartment, makes more room available for driver and passengers. The new *Deluxe* Ford V-8 cars have a new controlled ventilation system, Sealed-beam headlamps for safer night driving, softer springs both front and rear, an improved spring suspension, and a new tension bar ride stabilizer.

Emphasis in interior styling is on fine appointments. The *Coupe* type has a big parcel shelf behind the seat and a luggage compartment reached from inside the car, in addition to the big luggage compartment in the rear deck. A new *Deluxe Business Coupe* is also available. This differs from the *Coupe* in interior arrangement. The seat back is divided. The right side pivots forward to give access to a large compartment behind. This has auxiliary seats which fold down from each side for use of extra passengers. *N. W. Ayer & Son, September 15, 1939*

Babe Maggini, left, of Maggini Ford in San Francisco, and his salesman Frank Sherman, discuss a new '40 Ford *Deluxe Coupe* in this retouched advertising shot. For a few dollars extra, the buyer of this car got it equipped with optional radio, grille guard, and fog lights.

Right: It would be hard to resist trading in the old jalopy and paying $35 a month on this gorgeous '40 Ford *Deluxe Coupe*, shown at the introduction of the new models at Bennett Ford in Salt Lake City, October 6, 1939.

"I designed the tools myself . . . and then made them in the (Ford) shop. He (K. R. Wilson) took over after that. He would take my designs and put them into manufacturing, because he was making tools for service." FRED THOMS, FORD ENGINEER

A photograph taken for *Ford Times* magazine shows a 1940 Ford *Standard Tudor Sedan* getting headlight adjustment at the end of the assembly line in Dearborn. By now, Ford was making most of its own bodies, with Budd Company making about 20 percent (mostly commercial types), and Murray making about 15 percent. At this time, longtime body supplier Briggs was nearly out of the picture.

A colorful parts feeder line at Dearborn shows some of the commercial colors available in 1940. Head and taillight assemblies for all cars and trucks were produced at Ford's Flat Rock, Michigan, plant.

Below: The last step on the body line was the installation of accessories. At Dearborn, a worker prepares to place an optional radio in a nicely finished *Deluxe Coupe* body headed for final assembly.

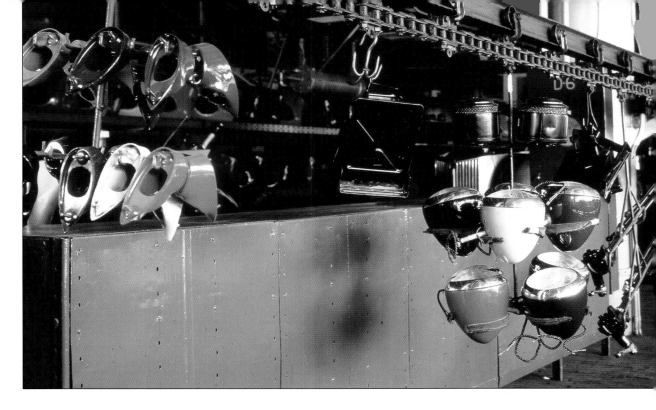

The endless stream of 1940 Ford models coming down the assembly line at the colossal Rouge plant in Dearborn, Michigan, poured out into the "B" Building for final inspection. Here, in a bedlam of noise and color, cars and trucks were started, headlights adjusted, hoods checked for fit, and other things fixed. At the far left, in front of a *Station Wagon*, and stake bed *Cab-Over-Engine Truck*, a Ford *Convertible Club Coupe* gets some attention.

Top left: A '40 Ford tow truck with a special body, and eye-catching color combination, gets its photo taken at Dearborn, before being delivered to a garage operator in Missouri.

Selling with a smile. Demon-strating the smartly-appointed Ford Deluxe Convertible Club Coupe's new automatic top at the 1940 Detroit Auto Show.

Left: The new '40 Fords, on display at the Company's famous Rotunda visitor center in Dearborn, includes a variety of enticing Fords, Mercurys, and Lincolns. Cars pictured include a *Deluxe Fordor Sedan*, a Ford *Deluxe Business Coupe*, and a Mercury *Town Sedan*.

". . . One day, I thought, let's make a steering wheel that you can look straight through and it's simple. You can put your hand on the spoke . . . Anyway Mr. Ford (Edsel) bought the idea, and we came out (1940) with that two-spoke steering wheel . . ." E. T. "BOB" GREGORIE, FORD CHIEF STYLIST

Gulf Coast Convertible Club members with their cars — all Fords — line up by year in a Sears Roebuck parking lot in Houston, June 22, 1940. They are about to be given a Texas Highway Patrol motorcycle escort through the city on their way to Galveston to promote "courteous and sane driving." Note the two-tone paint jobs, and aftermarket accessories which adorn some of the sporty '37-40 rag tops. No other car captured the heart of American youth in these years like the Fords which were by now being "customized" on a regular basis.

Left: The service department of Alsbury-Russell Ford in Houston August 11, 1940. A pair of brand new Ford convertible club coupes await dealer prep, while a *Deluxe Fordor Sedan* comes in for servicing. In the doorway is the shop's '40 Ford *Pickup.*

1940 FORD V-8 CONVERTIBLE CLUB COUPE

The Ford V-8 *Deluxe Convertible Club Coupe* for 1940 is a smart all-weather car with seats for five. A finger-tip gearshift on the steering post clears the front compartment and provides plenty of room for three passengers. An additional seat in the rear gives room for guests under the top. Seat cushions are of *Genuine Leather.* There is plenty of room in the luggage compartment for sports equipment. The top can be raised or lowered automatically. A new torsion bar ride-stabilizer contributes to easier steering. N. W. AYER & SON, SEPTEMBER 15, 1939

SPECIAL COLOR COMBINATIONS

It will be satisfactory for our assembly branches to furnish accessory-equipped units painted in the following color combinations when requested:
Folkestone Gray body with *Black* fenders and grille sides.
Folkestone Gray body with *Mandarin Maroon* fenders and grille sides.
Mandarin Maroon body with *Folkestone Gray* fenders and grille sides.
Cloud Mist Gray body with *Acadia Green* fenders and grille sides.
This applies to both Ford and Mercury units. FORD MOTOR COMPANY, DEARBORN, MICHIGAN, MAY 3, 1940

By 1940 the Ford *Station Wagon* had reached a superb level of workmanship, as represented by this *Deluxe* model on exhibit at a sportsman show in Los Angeles. Built of highly varnished maple, birch, and basswood at Ford's Iron Mountain plant in the hardwood forest of Michigan's Upper Peninsula, these cars were the ultimate for use around estates, lodges and resorts. Priced at around $1,000, this one is nicely equipped with accessory fog lamps, radio, and sideview mirror.

Top inset: Edsel Ford was the brilliance behind the first Ford station wagons in 1929. "He had a keen mentality," said his personal secretary, A. J. Lepine. "An outstanding thing about Mr. Ford was bright, observing, intelligent eyes."

A photo for the cover of *Ford News* magazine illustrates how owning a new '40 Mercury *Sport Convertible* was an invitation to the open road. This car has the optional *Red Leather* seats, which also came in *Brown Leather*. Another choice was a *Tan-gray* or *Black* fabric top, which stowed neatly beneath a matching boot. All bodies for this model were built at Ford's Lincoln plant.

Below: A bonny lass at the wheel of a new '40 Mercury *Sport Convertible* at Brae Burn Country Club in Houston, January 24, 1940.

THE '41-42 FORD-MERCURYS

The 1941 Fords were designed to share a common body with the Mercury, which was four-inches longer from the dash forward. The commonality of stampings was a key element in Edsel's overall strategy to make more parts interchangeable. "We could (now) put on different fenders," explained the veteran body engineer Joe Galamb,". . . a different hood, grille, and different size of wheels and so on."

As usual, chassis engineering came first — then the body designs — which were always initiated by Bob Gregorie who would begin a multitude of sketches before Edsel came in to tell him which of them he liked or didn't like. From the most promising sketches, the studio would then make a clay model and start work on different front-end and back-end ideas.

Gregorie enjoyed Edsel's regular visits to his studio. "He loved to come in and sit on the end of a drawing board and have me pick up an old blueprint and sketch something on the back — a hood ornament or some damn thing," recalled Gregorie, who by now had worked enjoyably with Edsel for most of a decade. "He'd say, 'All right, let's do it that way, huh? Does it look good to you, okay?' I really didn't realize what had taken place until after the thing was underway. With his okay, it surely kept things simple.

"Edsel liked to criticize the first model made in clay. First of all, we made a small sketch and then we made a clay model of it. He would criticize that . . . he didn't like the shape of the grille or the back end or the fender, or so on. He criticized the interior quite a lot, and the instrument work. When we made the first sample, Edsel criticized the trimming and the material we used. He was very particular about the cushions we used. He was also very particular about the riding qualities of the car. He knew what he wanted and insisted that he get it. When he made suggestions, we didn't make a new clay model, we just made the changes on the one we had. He would come back two or three days after to inspect it again. Everything was ready after he Okayed it to make up the final drawing for a sample. He never made any changes after we had our sample made up."

But there were always those engineering and production people nosing around the design studio. "So I was proceeding to put the final touches on this front end model," complained Gregorie about a typical visit, "and getting ready to apply aluminum foil for the plated parts of the grille when . . . I turned around, and here's the whole top echelon of the company marching in to take a look at this '41 Ford front-end. There was Charlie Sorensen, and he was a tall, blonde, handsome guy — tanned . . . and Larry Sheldrick, who was chief engineer at the time, and A. M. Wibel, who was boss of purchasing . . . Then Sorensen picks up my clay knife . . . and he starts drawing lines on the front fender, because they were trying to figure out how the hell they could make this thing. . . . And I'm in back of him muttering that Sorensen is ruining my model. . . ."

"So what happened," said stylist Bud Adams, explaining in his own memoirs the '41 Ford's peculiar front fender architecture, "was that it was decided to make it in three pieces. There was a horizontal feature line — a little groove — that

Right: **In a photo for the cover of** *Ford News* **the mighty Rouge plant in Dearborn makes a monumental backdrop for one of its latest products, a nicely tailored '41 Ford** *Super Deluxe Convertible Club Coupe.*

"... Some other projects I worked on were ... the 1941 front-end ... and such detail items as the brake pedal rubber pads and gear shift lever knobs ..." EUGENE G. "BUD" ADAMS, FORD STYLIST

An extreme early design idea for the '42 Ford front-end is tried on a new '41 model. Edsel would criticize the work in clay and changes would be made until it evolved into exactly what he wanted. Because of his sudden death in 1943, the 1942 car line would be the last approved by this great natural stylist. There would be no '43-45 models because of World War II.

ran from the back of the fender up to the center of the headlight, and then there was a vertical cut line right over the center line of the wheel in the side view."

The tension between Ford engineering and styling had sharpened toward the end of the 1940s. By now those who worked closely with Edsel began noticing that he was becoming more cynical and less enthused about his job. The problem as all could see, was his overbearing father Henry who, returning to his old ways, seemed to get a kick out of countermanding his son's every order.

The mind games caused Edsel to lose much of his creative spirit. "He seemed to have the attitude, 'Oh, what's the use? I'll go along with it,' " recalled Ford engineer, Emil Zoerlein. But there was more to it. What Zoerlein and the others didn't know was that Edsel was becoming terribly worn down and sick from the many long hours after Pearl Harbor, working to get Ford into full 1942 war production. "He never would complain," said Zoerlein, "or say anything even if he felt poorly . . . His very bad illness at the last came as a surprise to me. . . . I don't think anyone around the office knew a great deal about what ailed him."

Edsel had taken some time off to rest at his beach house in Florida during March 1943, and when he returned to work, dropped by to see Bob Gregorie in his design studio. "Some of these things (post-war car designs) which were done in '42 and '43 . . . were ready for presentation to Edsel," recalled the Ford chief stylist, "and then he just came in that one day. As a matter of fact, he didn't even see the models. . . . He said he was feeling badly, and he was going home. . . That was the last time I saw him."

Edsel B. Ford died at his home at Lake St. Clair Shores, Michigan, on May 26, 1943, of stomach cancer — and some would say of a broken heart because he could never please his father. He was 49.

In retrospect, after Edsel died, longtime Ford engineer Gene Farkas thought old Henry really did have deep feelings for his son but didn't know how to express them. "I think he admired him very much," he said. "I think he was trying to educate Edsel the hard way and didn't know when to stop . . . Anyway, he felt awful." ◆

"Mr. (Edsel) Ford was essentially an even-tempered man. . . . One would practically never hear him say anything sarcastic or resentful about other people . . . He did have a sense of humor. He had a way of chuckling at things that would be amusing. He had a quick laugh and a bright smile . . ." A. J. LEPINE, EDSEL'S PERSONAL SECRETARY

Edsel Ford 1893–1943

Edsel Ford's unexpected death in the spring of 1943 ended a brilliant chapter in American automotive design and cast a cloud over the company's stying department for years to come.

1941 FORDS INTRODUCED

New in every respect, the Ford V-8 for 1941 — the *Deluxe,* and *Super Deluxe* — was introduced in September in more than 6,000 Ford dealerships throughout the United States.

The *Super Deluxe* is available in six distinctive body types: *Tudor Sedan, Coupe, Convertible Club Coupe,* new *Sedan Coupe, Fordor Sedan* and *Station Wagon.* The lower-priced *Deluxe* Ford V-8 for 1941, which differs from the *Super Deluxe* in details of finish and appointments, is available as a *Fordor Sedan, Tudor Sedan* and *Coupe.* The *Station Wagon* is also available as a *Deluxe* type.

The exterior appearance of the car has been enhanced by placing the bright chrome door handles on the rustless steel trim line, which accentuates the length of this year's larger bodies. The radiator hood lock is now controlled by a handle inside the car, under the instrument panel, to the left of the driver.

In one of two *Coupe* models, the seat back pivots forward, permitting entrance to the rear compartment where auxiliary seats fold down for two more passengers. In the second *Coupe* model the seat back is hinged at the top and lifts upward from the bottom to permit access to the commodious luggage compartment.

The automatic top on the *Super Deluxe Convertible Club Coupe* is operated by electric motors instead of vacuum and operates even when the engine is not running. The wide, comfortable rear seat, brought in under the top, makes this an all-weather car for six-passengers. FORD NEWS, OCTOBER 1940

White seemed to be the special color of choice for showcasing the new '41 Fords. Here, dealers get their first close-up look at the features of a *Sedan Coupe* at a preview held at the company's Broadway showroom in New York City.

At the Long Beach, California, assembly plant Ford General Sales Manager John R. Davis, right, examines a new '41 Ford *Super Deluxe Fordor Sedan*, finished in *White* show color for the introduction of new models.

Below: One of the first '41 Mercurys, a two-door *Sedan*, is assembled at Dearborn, Michigan, October 25, 1940.

The handsome office staff of Titus Motors in Tacoma, Washington, is all set for business on introduction day of the new 1941 Ford models in October 1940. Visible beyond on the salesfloor is a *Pickup* and a pair of sedans.

Below: A '41 Ford *Super Deluxe Fordor Sedan*, finished in radical full-body *White* two-tone paint scheme, graces the showroom of a Houston, dealer. It was a special color combination meant to test the usually cautious Ford buyers market.

At Dearborn, chief stylist Bob Gregorie looks over the original '41 Ford paint scheme that led to production of some flashy cars like that on the opposite page. Only Edsel's more conservative views held back the dapper Gregorie who was burning with ideas. "This man was totally different," said one of his stylists. "He had an air; he had something to sell, and you could feel it!"

"... General Motors was offering more variety and color. We were concerned about color in some of the design nuances that we wanted to do and couldn't ... There were a lot of designs that were protected with patent rights ... It gave us a car compatible with competition, at least ..." TUCKER MADAWICK, FORD STYLIST

Burly football players for the University of Detroit, and their coach, pose with a flashy *White* '41 Mercury *Convertible*. A bit wider than the Ford, the Mercury had more shoulder room – a selling point that was gaining popularity.

Below: Portland, Oregon's Rose Festival Queen, Betty Jane Harding, poses prettily with the car that will carry her in the downtown parade. The youthful new '41 Mercury *Convertible*, specially ordered in the traditional *White* festival color, was provided by the local dealer Wolfard & Francis, and is sported–up for the event with such extras as fender skirts, and whitewall tires.

QUEEN BETTY JANE

PORTLAND ROSE FESTIVAL ASSOCIATION

S&C Motors of San Francisco delivers a fleet of '41 Mercury Town Sedans to Driveurself, a local rental car company.

Below: One of the early '41 Mercury *Sedan Coupe* models comes off the line at Dearborn October 11, 1940.

New '41 Fords of every description cover the grounds of Wazee Farmer's Market near downtown Denver, Colorado, ready for a big summer sales extravaganza. It was the combined promotion of six Denver-area Ford dealers, who ordered a full trainload of everything from the top selling sedans, to convertibles, and trucks. At the near left one of the dealers, and his family, stand next to a coupe model just before the grand opening.

This accessory exhibit in the showroom of the Ford assembly plant in Long Beach, California, January 4, 1941, was to show visiting dealers how to use a display merchandiser to sell the profitable add-ons.

By now, customers were well accustomed to time payments, and for a few more dollars they could get a wide range of items on their cars, from radios, and oil filters, to fenders skirts, and fog lights.

STATION WAGONS

Hollywood screen idol Tyrone Power takes delivery of a new Ford *Super Deluxe Station Wagon* from a Los Angeles dealer. The next stop was the sign painter to put the name of his rancho on the door — like the one on actress Gloria Swanson's '36 Ford wagon which read, *Casa de las Estrellas*, "House of the Stars." That car would find its way into the good hands of California V-8 collector, Charlie Bennett.

The good old custom of the Roaring Twenties when jalopies were given the personal touch of a name is being revived on a high hat plane.

Many station wagons which serve the smart estates of America now receive this mark of owner esteem. Painted on door or body panels, the names may range from the (brick) implications of "Swifty" or "Whoopenholler" to the dignified titles of the estates themselves.

A recent survey by Lincoln and Mercury dealers indicate that estate names predominate on Mercury station wagons. Among them are Century Oaks, Deep Hollow, Red Gable Farms, The Brambles, Ridgeway, Shore Acres, Highwood and Vista Del Vale. Throughout the West it was found that wealthy ranch owners often identify station wagons by burning their registered range brands into the panel wood. FORD NEWS DEPARTMENT, DECEMBER 1941

Inset right: Owners of a gas station in Tracys Landing, Maryland, pose proudly with their freshly signed and two-toned new '41 Ford *Pickup.*

Inset far right: The attractive '41 Ford *134-inch Panel Delivery* used to service customers of a Pasadena, California, Ford dealer. This model could also be ordered with dual rear wheels.

Right: Eighty-one new '41 Ford pickups, and miscellaneous truck models, stand ready to bring on the buyers at a lot in Dodge City, Kansas. In May of that year Ford Motor Company announced that it would soon offer a Six-Cylinder engine option to the regular 90-hp V-8 in all *Deluxe* and *Super Deluxe* Ford passenger car types, as well as commercial cars and trucks. It was Ford's first "Six" since 1906.

". . . Mr. (Henry) Ford did let them come out with a Six. I imagine he did this to get the sales up higher. He told me . . . that there was only about twelve dollars difference in cost . . . but you can get eighty more dollars for (a car) with an Eight. The people demand a Six because they think the service is less . . . but it isn't. The power flow is so much nicer and better on an Eight. . ." FRED THOMS, FORD ENGINEER

217

Models in the latest fashions help glamorize the new 1942 Ford-Lincoln-Mercury passenger car line at a formal Kansas City stage presentation, complete with orchestra, September 24, 1941.

Left: A Houston crowd with a slight case of war jitters takes a close look at one of the new '42 Ford *Special Tudor* sedans that has been reduced to the basics in trim and appointments. By now, war clouds were gathering; the Germans were spreading out across Europe, and the Japanese were threatening the Pacific. Ford Motor Company was already building jeeps, and tooling up to build B-24 bombers. Amid rumors of a coming world conflict, chrome and other materials had suddenly become scarce and the new Ford cars showed it.

FORD CARS FOR '42 NOW IN SHOWROOMS

Safety and economy are stressed in the new Ford cars for 1942, which are now on special display in dealer showrooms.

The new Ford is powered with either an advanced six-cylinder engine, or the famous V-8. Either of the optional Ford engines delivers 90-horsepower. Their performance is even higher than before, and operating economy has been improved through a long series of engineering refinements.

Featuring new exterior lines and new styling within, the 1942 Ford car is lower, safer, and easier riding than any of its more than 29-million predecessors.

Although production of 1942 Ford cars will be sharply curtailed as the immense program of defense work being carried out by the company gets into full swing, Ford engineers declare the new cars are unquestionably the finest in the 38 years of the company's history. While some new materials have replaced old ones because of defense requirements, the change has meant added manufacturing cost rather than any let-down in service or appearance of the parts affected.

Three lines of Ford cars are offered – the *Super Deluxe,* the *Deluxe* and the economy *Special.* The first two are equipped at the factory with either the "Six" or 8-cylinder engine. The *Special* is offered with the six-cylinder power plant only.

In appearance the new cars are larger and more massive. A completely new frontal design flows smoothly into the body lines to accentuate the general streamlined effect of the car's styling.

There are six *Super Deluxe* body types, including a *Convertible Club Coupe,* and an eight-passenger *Station Wagon.* The *Super Deluxe* cars are available with a choice of six colors, all in durable Ford baked synthetic enamel.

Deluxe car body types are the *Tudor* sedan, *Fordor* sedan, *Coupe* and a new *Sedan Coupe,* with a choice of three colors, while the *Special* body types are *Coupe,* and *Tudor* and *Fordor* sedans. The *Special* comes in *Black* only. FORD NEWS, OCTOBER 1941

Ready for the crowds at the Kansas City, Missouri, introduction of the full 1942 Ford-Lincoln-Mercury line September 24, 1941. This was a company event, presented by the local Kansas City Ford assembly plant. There are no convertibles in the photo because they were a hard sell here in the winter months, but mainly because the soft top bodies were usually the last to be put into production. The 1942 models were extremely rare, it being a six-month production year. Less than five months after this photo was taken, all U.S. civilian auto production was stopped, and the factories turned to the war effort.

Inset Top Right: Because of the production shutdown caused by World War II, just 956 of the new '42 Mercury Club Convertibles were produced — making them among the rarest of all Ford Motor Company soft-tops.

A salesman at Edgemont Ford, a small dealership in Tracys Landing, Maryland, poses proudly with a new *Super Deluxe Fordor Sedan* just before the February 10, 1942 government order stopping all U.S. automobile production. It would be his last new car delivery for the duration of World War II.

Top left: The smoothly-crafted '42 Ford *Super Deluxe Station Wagon* was another beauty from the styling genius of Edsel Ford and Bob Gregorie, but because of the war-shortened production year, fewer than 6,000 of them were built.

Opposite: A '42 Ford *Special Tudor Sedan* on exhibit at the Ford Rotunda in Dearborn. The *Special* models came only in *Black* color, with the 6-cylinder engine.

THE '46-48 FORD-MERCURYS

More than any other American automaker, World War II was a calamity for Ford Motor Company. First came the turmoil caused by the change from domestic vehicle — to war production in 1942. This was followed by the tragic loss of talent and family leadership when Edsel died in 1943. Then old Henry became increasingly senile, and let his enforcer Harry Bennett pull off a power-hungry plot to rid the company of anyone with influence. Among the top men forced out was the able Ford chief engineer Larry Sheldrick, followed by chief stylist Bob Gregorie. Chief of production "Cast-iron Charlie" Sorensen, with Henry since 1905, was next — resigning under pressure in early 1944.

The loss of Gregorie hit his men particularly hard. "Edsel Ford had a tremendous amount of confidence in Gregorie and his ability and his decisions," reminisced stylist Emmett O'Rear. "Right after Edsel died they (Bennett's men) really did a number on the design shop." Gregorie's reaction to the whole mess was to quit, leaving an assistant, Eric Ramstrum, to carry on in his place. In progress was the styling of the post-war Fords — the last influenced to some extent by Edsel.

Then in 1945, after Edsel's young son Henry Ford II was recalled from the Navy to take the company's helm from his ailing grandfather, the situation regained some normalcy. Bennett was kicked out, Gregorie came back as chief stylist, and the company began work to get the first post-war American cars into production.

Why Ford was able to get a jump on the rest of the industry in post-war domestic car production is attributed to the large and virtually complete bank of '42 parts kept in storage all through the war. By making use of these on the new '46 Ford, and giving it the barest of improvements such as new brakes, better springs, a reinforced frame and ten more horsepower, production problems were held to the parts needed for the car's modestly re-worked styling.

The first post-war Ford — a *Super Deluxe Tudor* — was built at Dearborn July 3, 1945, and was delivered later by Henry Ford II as a personal gift to President Harry S. Truman at the White House. It was a full month before the formal surrender of Japan.

There would still be awhile though before regular citizens would see any of the new '46 Fords. That day would come on October 26, 1945, when, according to *Business Week*, ". . . (the cars) . . . were suddenly unveiled to a lip-smacking, car-hungry public." Ford publicists would call it "V-8 Day" when, "millions of businessmen, housewives, stenographers, eager servicemen, and curious kids flocked to the Ford dealers' showrooms for their first look at a post-war car." But it was just a mouth-watering look. The dealers could only take orders until the O.P.A (Office of Price Administration) set the sales price to prevent profiteering. By law, first in line to get new cars would be returning war veterans and people and businesses in essential services.

Meanwhile, Gregorie was back to work in his old design studio building the clay concepts of the Ford-Lincoln-Mercury cars that would replace the first post-war series. During this time, he also managed to get the last of Edsel's idea cars off the sketchpad and into production. It was the stunning new *"Sportsman"* series of Ford and Mercury convertibles designed to spark the market for a soft-top in the station wagon class. Featuring wood bodies, beautifully handcrafted of bent maple and mahogany, the cars would be produced in very limited numbers and were intended for those who could afford to pamper them. Gregorie admitted that they were really "quite fragile" and

Right: **Students at P. S. du Pont High School in Wilmington, Delaware, see their first postwar Ford, a 1946 *Super Deluxe Tudor Sedan*, October 26, 1945. A brand-new automobile was a novelty to most Americans who hadn't seen one since early 1942, when the nation's passenger car production was converted to the war effort.**

Henry Ford, the mechanical genius who became America's first billionaire, died April 7, 1947. Here, at an earlier time, he talks with his grandson Henry Ford II whose father Edsel died in 1943. Young Henry would become president and while a strong leader, had little eye for design. This led to confusion and the resignation of chief stylist Bob Gregorie in December 1946.

"...After Edsel passed, we could definitely see a slipping in both his (Henry's) memory and his mental facilities. He wouldn't react as quickly as he did before..." GENE FARKAS, FORD EXPERIMENTAL ENGINEER

"An enterprise is fortunate that can find in the founder's line the abilities to carry it forward... Those who knew him best see in Henry Ford II a worthy scion of his distinguished grandfather." DETROIT NEWS, Sept. 22, 1945.

Right: A section of Ford styling July 3, 1945 — the day the company rolled off its first '46 post-war model. In progress by Bob Gregorie and his stylists can be seen several prototypes which became the '49 Lincoln-Mercurys.

Top right: A clay prototype '46 Ford *Tudor Sedan* June 1, 1944.

impractical. "You couldn't take them out in the weather," he confessed. "You had to keep them varnished."

The Sportsman series was Bob Gregorie's last full styling classic at Ford. In December 1946, he quit the company for good. His heart just wasn't in his work. For months he had been struggling with some "fastback" design concepts for the next generation of Ford cars but was bogged down without someone like Edsel to give him a clear direction. Young Henry didn't know anything about car styling — didn't like his clay models — and didn't know what to tell him. So, well-known Detroit industrial designer George W. Walker was brought in as a consultant and the understandably insulted Gregorie resigned. Hired in his place was Tom Hibbard from General Motors.

An era had come to an end. Edsel and Gregorie were gone, and on April 7, 1947, Henry Ford died at his home in Dearborn, Michigan, at age 83.

Ironically, while George Walker directed the styling of the wildly successful '49 Ford models, Bob Gregorie's designs in progress were too good to be scrapped. His last clays became the basis for the sensational new '49 Lincolns and Mercurys.◆

228

1946 FORDS ANNOUNCED

Local cowgirl Carlyn Cox got the first '46 Ford *Super Deluxe Convertible Club Coupe* delivered at Murray-Young Motors in Midland, Texas.

Left: Officially, the first public delivery of a new '46 Ford was to U.S. Army Lt. John Sjogen, shown receiving it in October 1945. Returning war veterans got top priority. The cars were ready earlier but were held up until the government set the price. Ford dealers got cars in proportion to their 1941 sales.

"At that time they could sell anything with four wheels and an engine in it." FORD WORKER, 1946

The Ford Motor Company will build about 40,000 of the industry's over-all allotment of 200,000 cars in 1945. The new Ford is not a "stop-gap" model hurriedly produced, but is the result of four years of research and production during the War, company officials said.

It contains more mechanical improvements than were included in any previous year-to-year model. Outstanding features of the car are: a more powerful engine, better performance, longer life, improved economy and a better ride. The new V-8 engine develops 100-horsepower. Pre-war Fords were equipped with V-8 engines developing 90-horsepower.

The chief exterior change is a newly designed radiator grille. Luxury and eye-appeal are accentuated in the interiors. Instrumentation is generally the same, but the styling and color schemes of the instrument panel are new.

An improved ride and better roadability, especially at high speeds in cross winds or on curves, is assured by the use of improved-type springs and shock absorbers, and the addition of a rear-end sway bar. The thickness of the spring leaves has been reduced and their number increased.

The brakes are new and require less pedal pressure. They are easier to adjust and feature a floating type shoe that seats itself.

A new standard in fuel economy has been achieved despite an increase in horsepower. Higher engine compression, a change in the engine-axle ratio, and the adoption of a new carburetor has made this possible. *FORD MOTOR COMPANY, PUBLIC RELATIONS OFFICE, NEW YORK, NEW YORK*

"The chassis wasn't changed very much on the V-8. It wasn't even changed after the war. The only change we made was reinforcing the frame all the time. The frame was twisting and tearing the bodies apart." JOE GALAMB

Assemblers "drop" a V-8 engine into a 1946 Ford passenger car chassis at the Kansas City, Missouri, assembly plant. Ford began producing automobiles here in 1912. During World War II, production was turned to military types and then in 1946, to cars and trucks again.

Right: A load of new Fords, including a pair of Super Deluxe Coupes, a *Pickup,* and a *Super Deluxe Convertible Club Coupe,* prepare to leave the assembly plant in Long Beach, California, April 9, 1946. After crippling strikes and parts shortages, the company was finally getting into full postwar production.

To promote sales, Ford had an entire Hollywood publicity department devoted to getting the post-war models in the movies where the public could see them in action. This high-toned '46 Mercury *Station Wagon* starred in Universal's "Mr. Peabody and the Mermaid," with William Powell and Irene Hervey.

Ford was one of the first U.S. automakers to resume operations in war-torn Europe. A handsome Mercury *Sedan Coupe*, sporting a set of "Kleber Colombes" whitewalls, competes for attention at the 1946 Paris Auto Show.

Top right: The first Ford *Sportsman* was sold to actress Ella Raines in Hollywood on Christmas Day, 1945, after being driven by Henry Ford II and displayed in Dearborn. Miss Raines, pictured, had her initials monogrammed on its doors.

Just 723 of these cars were built in 1946 and another 200 of the more expensive Mercury models. Production of these rather fragile types was discontinued in November 1947.

1946

NEW FORD SPORTSMAN

A parade float carries one of Ford's stunning new Super Deluxe Sportsman Convertibles during the June 1946, Detroit "Golden Jubilee" to celebrate the automobile industry's 50 years of progress. The car, with its highly-varnished all-wood-paneled body, was the last of the Bob Gregorie-designed Fords.

A *"Sportsman Convertible"* has been added to the 1946 Ford line. This car, with the appearance of a station wagon, and the convertible top and close-coupled seating of a convertible coupe, will be in limited production. The wooden panels of the new body are applied over a steel frame. The power-operated top used on the *Convertible Club Coupe,* and the standard-type window risers, and other fittings are utilized. Inside, the car will be furnished with *Leather* upholstery. FORD MOTOR COMPANY, SEPTEMBER 13, 1945

It was still the postwar seller's market so, in April 1947 — with a few minor changes, such as relocated round parking lights, a new hood medallion, wider stainless belt trim, new interior trim, and colors, etc., — the '46 Fords simply became the '47 models. Here, at Tom Boyd Ford in Dearborn, Michigan, a salesmen makes a deal on one of the sporty new-model Super Deluxe Convertible Club Coupes.

Opposite: Slightly re-designed '47 Fords and Mercurys move through final inspection lines at the Driveaway Build-ing at Dearborn Assembly. From here they would be delivered or driven home by car-starved dealers, where vehicles were so slow in arriving from the factory that good used models often sold at new car prices.

Rising Hollywood film star Wanda Hendrix takes delivery of a new sport light-equipped '47 Mercury *Convertible Coupe* from C. K. Marley, the Lincoln-Mercury dealer in her hometown of Jacksonville, Florida.

Left: A dazzling new *Sportsman Convertible Coupe* rotates on a turntable inside the Ford tent at the Del Mar County Fair near San Diego, California, during the summer of 1947. The ultimate in sportiness, and loaded with accessories, the car was made for this part of the country — known for its sunny climate, horse tracks, ranchos, and movie star estates. Other Fords on display include some trucks, and a *Panel Delivery*.

237

A worker sprays varnish on the roof slats of a Ford station wagon body at the company's big Iron Mountain, Michigan, plant in 1947. From here the bodies would go through a bake oven for final finish before being fitted with seats and hardware for shipment to assembly plants worldwide.

A White *Deluxe Sedan Coupe* is the star at Ford Dearborn, November 4, 1947, as all action stops for a publicity shot to show the new '48 Ford models coming off the line. Until that day they were all 1947 models. The only difference in the cars was a new engine prefix, "1948'" on the title, and a new 3-position ignition lock. It was an action to buy time until the all-new '49 models were ready in June.

TO ALL FORD OFFICES

Engine and model numbers for 1948 (Ford) cars — the lowest number used with 1948 prefixes for six-cylinder passenger car engines is 87HA-0536. Lowest number used with 1948 prefixes for V-8 passenger car engines is 899A-1984859. Due to inventory of engines at various assembly plants, some 1947 models will have higher numbers than the above. However, the prefix changes will definitely identify the 1948 models from the 1947 models. FORD MOTOR COMPANY, NOVEMBER 4, 1947

Proud Canadians wanted to be different so Ford Dearborn designed a new post-war "Mercury" nameplate commercial line just for them, with a unique front-end and other features. This '48 *One-Ton Truck* V-8 model, just delivered at a Victoria, British Columbia, dealer, shows the "one-size-fits-all" oddly mismatched front-end unique to the wider-fendered truck line. On lighter models such as the pickup the headlight section matched the fenders.

Opposite: The Queen of the 1948 Portland, Oregon, Rose Festival poses in her classy new Mercury *Convertible Coupe* with her escort at a scenic overlook. The car, finished in traditional factory *White* show color, was provided by Francis & Hopkins the Ford dealer in Portland.

The low-cost, dependable, post-war Fords were hot-sellers on the resale market. A night salesman at a Cincinnati, Ohio, car lot in late 1948 makes a carnival-like pitch on a slightly used '47 Ford sedan.

Right: The first of the newly designed *F-Series* Ford trucks were introduced in 1948. A pair of the all-new *Pickup* models, custom-equipped for service duty, are pictured at City Lincoln-Mercury in Pasadena, California. Among the sharp-looking used cars on the sales lot here can be seen a '46 Ford *Station Wagon*, at the far right, and a '47 Mercury *Convertible*, at the near right.

An accessory-loaded new '48 Ford *Super Deluxe Convertible Club Coupe* graces the showroom window of Tom Boyd Ford in Dearborn, Michigan, during the Christmas holidays of 1947 — the perfect surprise gift to put a little sparkle in that romance. The price was about $1,635 FOB Detroit.

Opposite: A Kansas City, Missouri, crowd mobs a Ford *Super Deluxe Convertible Club Coupe* at Broadway Motors during a spring dealer promotion to clear out the 1948 models. It was the last chance to buy one of these popular V-8s before the yet-to-be-described new '49 Fords would make their showroom debut in June.

With news that the completely-new '49 Ford models would soon be coming to showrooms, dealers began offering good deals to clear out the '48s. This advertising shot at Broadway Motors in Kansas City, Missouri, shows how easy it is to get one of the last Super Deluxe Fordor Sedans in stock. Just a week earlier, on April 2, 1948, the first of the low-slung, slab-sided '49s began rolling off the assembly lines to begin a whole new chapter of FAMOUS FORD V-8s.

Opposite: At the big Rouge assembly plant in Dearborn, Michigan, new '48 Ford and Mercury models, including coupes, sedans, convertibles and station wagons, stand in the dealer haulaway yard ready to fulfill many an American dream. ◆